50 Israel Bread Recipes for Home

By: Kelly Johnson

Table of Contents

- Challah
- Pita
- Lachuch
- Jachnun
- Bagels
- Sambusak
- Matbucha Bread
- Khubz
- Tachina Bread
- Zaatar Bread
- Sabich Sandwich Bread
- Rye Bread
- Israeli Focaccia
- Pita with Hummus
- Flatbread
- Cheese Bourekas
- Spinach Bourekas
- Sweet Challah
- Oregano Bread
- Onion Bread
- Barley Bread
- Herb Flatbread
- Sesame Bagels
- Fennel Seed Bread
- Tomato Bread
- Green Olive Bread
- Date and Nut Bread
- Coriander Flatbread
- Sweet Potato Bread
- Garlic Bread
- Cinnamon Bread
- Whole Wheat Pita

- Pumpkin Bread
- Caramelized Onion Bread
- Mediterranean Bread
- Rosemary Focaccia
- Lavash
- Sun-Dried Tomato Bread
- Coconut Bread
- Sourdough Pita
- Quinoa Bread
- Poppy Seed Challah
- Kamut Bread
- Zucchini Bread
- Sweet Cornbread
- Crispy Flatbread
- Herbed Focaccia
- Spelt Bread
- Olive Bread
- Almond Bread

Challah

Ingredients:

- 1 cup warm water (110°F or 45°C)
- 1 packet (2¼ tsp) active dry yeast
- ¼ cup granulated sugar
- 4 cups all-purpose flour
- 1½ tsp salt
- 1/3 cup vegetable oil
- 2 large eggs
- 1 egg yolk (for egg wash)
- 1 tbsp water (for egg wash)
- Poppy seeds or sesame seeds (optional, for topping)

Instructions:

1. **Activate the Yeast:**
    - In a small bowl, dissolve 1 tablespoon of sugar in warm water. Sprinkle the yeast over the top and let sit for 5-10 minutes, until frothy.
2. **Mix the Dough:**
    - In a large bowl, combine the remaining sugar, flour, and salt.
    - Add the yeast mixture, vegetable oil, and 2 eggs. Mix until the dough begins to come together.
3. **Knead:**
    - Turn the dough onto a floured surface and knead for about 8-10 minutes, until smooth and elastic. The dough should be slightly sticky but manageable.
4. **First Rise:**
    - Place the dough in a lightly oiled bowl, cover, and let rise in a warm place for 1-1½ hours, or until doubled in size.
5. **Shape the Challah:**
    - Punch down the dough and divide it into three equal parts. Roll each part into a long rope, about 12-14 inches long.
    - Braid the three ropes together, pinching the ends to seal. Place the braided loaf onto a greased baking sheet or a parchment-lined baking sheet.
6. **Second Rise:**
    - Cover the loaf loosely with plastic wrap or a clean kitchen towel and let rise for 30-45 minutes, or until it has risen and is puffy.
7. **Prepare for Baking:**
    - Preheat your oven to 375°F (190°C).
    - In a small bowl, whisk together the egg yolk and 1 tablespoon of water to create an egg wash. Brush this mixture over the loaf.

8. **Add Toppings:**
    - If desired, sprinkle poppy seeds or sesame seeds on top of the loaf.
9. **Bake:**
    - Bake for 25-30 minutes, or until the bread is golden brown and sounds hollow when tapped on the bottom.
10. **Cool:**
    - Let the Challah cool on a wire rack before slicing.

This Challah is perfect for enjoying on its own, with butter, or as part of a meal. It's slightly sweet and has a soft, airy crumb with a beautiful golden crust. Enjoy!

Pita

Ingredients:

- 1½ cups warm water (110°F or 45°C)
- 1 packet (2¼ tsp) active dry yeast
- 1 tbsp granulated sugar
- 3½ cups all-purpose flour
- 1½ tsp salt
- 2 tbsp olive oil

Instructions:

1. **Activate the Yeast:**
    - In a small bowl, dissolve sugar in warm water. Sprinkle yeast over the top and let sit for 5-10 minutes, until frothy.
2. **Mix the Dough:**
    - In a large bowl, combine flour and salt.
    - Add the yeast mixture and olive oil. Mix until a dough forms.
3. **Knead:**
    - Turn the dough onto a floured surface and knead for about 8-10 minutes, until smooth and elastic.
4. **First Rise:**
    - Place the dough in a lightly oiled bowl, cover, and let rise in a warm place for 1-1½ hours, or until doubled in size.
5. **Shape the Pita:**
    - Punch down the dough and divide it into 8-10 equal pieces.
    - Roll each piece into a flat circle, about ¼-inch thick.
6. **Preheat Oven:**
    - Preheat your oven to 475°F (245°C). Place a baking sheet or pizza stone in the oven to heat.
7. **Bake:**
    - Place rolled-out dough circles onto the hot baking sheet or pizza stone.
    - Bake for 2-3 minutes, or until the pita puffs up and is lightly golden.
8. **Cool:**
    - Remove the pita from the oven and let cool on a wire rack.

Pita Bread is great for sandwiches, wraps, or dipping. Enjoy your homemade pitas fresh from the oven!

Lachuch

Ingredients:

- 2 cups all-purpose flour
- 1 cup whole wheat flour
- 1½ tsp baking powder
- 1 tsp salt
- 1½ cups warm water
- 1 cup sourdough starter (active and bubbly, or use 1 cup plain yogurt as a substitute)
- 1 tbsp honey (optional, for a touch of sweetness)

Instructions:

1. **Mix the Dough:**
   - In a large bowl, whisk together the all-purpose flour, whole wheat flour, baking powder, and salt.
   - Add the warm water, sourdough starter (or yogurt), and honey (if using). Mix until smooth.
2. **Let the Batter Rest:**
   - Cover the bowl with a clean kitchen towel and let the batter rest in a warm place for 1-2 hours. The batter should be bubbly and slightly thick.
3. **Preheat Skillet:**
   - Heat a non-stick skillet or griddle over medium-high heat. Lightly grease with oil if necessary.
4. **Cook the Lachuch:**
   - Pour about ½ cup of batter onto the hot skillet and spread it into a round shape. Cook for 2-3 minutes, or until bubbles form on the surface and the edges look set.
   - Flip and cook for another 1-2 minutes, or until lightly browned.
5. **Keep Warm:**
   - Place cooked lachuch on a plate covered with a kitchen towel to keep warm and soft. Continue with the remaining batter.
6. **Serve:**
   - Serve lachuch warm with your favorite toppings or as a side with soups, stews, or salads.

Lachuch has a unique texture and flavor that's perfect for scooping up sauces or simply enjoying with a bit of butter or jam. Enjoy this delicious Yemeni bread!

Jachnun

Ingredients:

- 4 cups all-purpose flour
- 1 cup warm water (110°F or 45°C)
- 1 packet (2¼ tsp) active dry yeast
- 2 tbsp sugar
- 1 tsp salt
- ½ cup vegetable oil or melted butter
- ¼ cup honey (optional, for a touch of sweetness)
- 1 egg (optional, for brushing)

Instructions:

1. **Activate the Yeast:**
    - In a small bowl, dissolve sugar in warm water. Sprinkle yeast over and let sit for 5-10 minutes, until frothy.
2. **Mix the Dough:**
    - In a large bowl, combine flour and salt.
    - Add the yeast mixture, vegetable oil (or melted butter), and honey (if using). Mix until a dough forms.
3. **Knead:**
    - Turn the dough onto a floured surface and knead for about 8-10 minutes, until smooth and elastic.
4. **First Rise:**
    - Place the dough in a lightly oiled bowl, cover, and let rise in a warm place for 1-1½ hours, or until doubled in size.
5. **Shape the Jachnun:**
    - Punch down the dough and divide it into 4 equal pieces.
    - Roll each piece into a thin rectangle, about ¼-inch thick. Brush lightly with oil or melted butter.
    - Roll each rectangle into a tight log, then coil the log into a spiral shape. Place each spiral into a greased baking dish.
6. **Second Rise:**
    - Cover the spirals and let them rise for about 30 minutes.
7. **Preheat Oven:**
    - Preheat your oven to 275°F (135°C).
8. **Bake:**
    - If using, brush the tops with beaten egg for a shiny finish.
    - Bake for 4-6 hours, or until the jachnun is deeply browned and has a soft, buttery texture.

9. **Cool:**
    - Let the jachnun cool slightly before serving.

Traditionally served for breakfast or on Shabbat, Jachnun pairs well with hard-boiled eggs, spicy tomato sauce, or fresh salads. Enjoy this rich, flavorful bread that's perfect for a leisurely meal!

Bagels

Ingredients:

For the Dough:

- 4 cups all-purpose flour
- 1 packet (2¼ tsp) active dry yeast
- 1½ cups warm water (110°F or 45°C)
- 1 tbsp granulated sugar
- 1½ tsp salt

For Boiling:

- 2 quarts water
- 2 tbsp granulated sugar (or 2 tbsp malt syrup, if available)

For Topping (optional):

- Sesame seeds
- Poppy seeds
- Coarse salt
- Everything bagel seasoning

Instructions:

1. **Activate the Yeast:**
    - In a small bowl, dissolve the sugar in warm water. Sprinkle the yeast over the top and let sit for 5-10 minutes, until frothy.
2. **Mix the Dough:**
    - In a large bowl, combine the flour and salt.
    - Add the yeast mixture and mix until a dough forms.
3. **Knead:**
    - Turn the dough onto a floured surface and knead for about 8-10 minutes, until smooth and elastic.
4. **First Rise:**
    - Place the dough in a lightly oiled bowl, cover, and let rise in a warm place for 1 hour, or until doubled in size.
5. **Shape the Bagels:**
    - Punch down the dough and divide it into 8-12 equal pieces, depending on the size of the bagels you want.
    - Roll each piece into a ball, then use your finger to poke a hole in the center and stretch it out to form a bagel shape.

6. **Prepare to Boil:**
   - Bring the water and sugar (or malt syrup) to a boil in a large pot. Reduce heat to a simmer.
7. **Boil the Bagels:**
   - Carefully drop a few bagels at a time into the simmering water. Boil for 1-2 minutes on each side. Use a slotted spoon to remove them and place them on a baking sheet.
8. **Add Toppings:**
   - If using toppings, sprinkle them on the bagels while they are still wet from boiling.
9. **Preheat Oven:**
   - Preheat your oven to 425°F (220°C).
10. **Bake:**
    - Bake the bagels for 20-25 minutes, or until they are golden brown.
11. **Cool:**
    - Let the bagels cool on a wire rack before slicing.

Bagels are perfect for sandwiches, toasts, or simply enjoyed with a spread of cream cheese. Enjoy your homemade bagels fresh from the oven!

Sambusak

Ingredients:

For the Dough:

- 2½ cups all-purpose flour
- 1 tsp salt
- 1 tsp baking powder
- ½ cup unsalted butter, chilled and cut into small pieces
- 1 cup plain yogurt (or sour cream)
- 1 egg yolk (for brushing, optional)

For the Filling:

- 1 tbsp olive oil
- 1 onion, finely chopped
- 1 cup cooked ground beef or lamb (or use a vegetarian filling like spinach and feta)
- 1 tsp ground cumin
- 1 tsp ground coriander
- ½ tsp paprika
- ¼ tsp ground cinnamon (optional)
- Salt and pepper to taste
- ¼ cup fresh parsley or cilantro, chopped (optional)

Instructions:

1. **Prepare the Dough:**
    - In a large bowl, combine flour, salt, and baking powder.
    - Add the chilled butter and rub it into the flour using your fingers or a pastry cutter until the mixture resembles coarse crumbs.
    - Stir in the yogurt until a dough forms. Knead briefly on a floured surface until smooth.
    - Cover the dough with plastic wrap and let it rest in the refrigerator for at least 30 minutes.
2. **Prepare the Filling:**
    - Heat olive oil in a skillet over medium heat. Add the chopped onion and cook until soft and translucent.
    - Add the cooked ground beef or lamb and the spices (cumin, coriander, paprika, and cinnamon). Cook for a few more minutes, stirring occasionally.
    - Season with salt and pepper, and stir in the chopped parsley or cilantro if using. Let the mixture cool.
3. **Assemble the Sambusak:**

- Preheat your oven to 375°F (190°C).
- Roll out the dough on a floured surface to about ¼-inch thickness.
- Cut the dough into circles (about 4-5 inches in diameter) using a cookie cutter or the rim of a glass.
- Place a spoonful of filling in the center of each circle.
- Fold the dough over to form a half-moon shape and press the edges to seal. You can crimp the edges with a fork for a decorative touch.

4. **Bake:**
    - Place the filled sambusak on a baking sheet lined with parchment paper.
    - Brush the tops with egg yolk if desired, for a golden finish.
    - Bake for 20-25 minutes, or until the sambusak are golden brown and crisp.

5. **Cool:**
    - Let the sambusak cool slightly before serving.

Sambusak can be served warm or at room temperature and pairs well with a variety of dips, such as yogurt or tahini sauce. Enjoy this delightful pastry!

Matbucha Bread

Ingredients:

For the Bread Dough:

- 3 cups all-purpose flour
- 1 packet (2¼ tsp) active dry yeast
- 1½ cups warm water (110°F or 45°C)
- 2 tbsp olive oil
- 1 tbsp sugar
- 1½ tsp salt

For the Matbucha Filling:

- 1 cup Matbucha (store-bought or homemade)
    - *To make Matbucha:*
        - 4 large tomatoes, peeled and chopped
        - 2 red bell peppers, chopped
        - 4 cloves garlic, minced
        - ¼ cup olive oil
        - 1 tsp paprika
        - ½ tsp ground cumin
        - ¼ tsp cayenne pepper (optional, for heat)
        - Salt and pepper to taste

Instructions:

1. **Prepare the Matbucha (if making from scratch):**
    - In a large skillet, heat olive oil over medium heat. Add garlic and cook until fragrant.
    - Add the chopped tomatoes and red bell peppers. Cook for about 10 minutes until the vegetables are soft.
    - Stir in paprika, cumin, cayenne pepper (if using), salt, and pepper.
    - Reduce the heat and cook for another 20-30 minutes, stirring occasionally, until the mixture is thick and spreadable.
    - Let the Matbucha cool.
2. **Prepare the Bread Dough:**
    - In a small bowl, dissolve sugar in warm water. Sprinkle yeast over the top and let sit for 5-10 minutes, until frothy.
    - In a large bowl, combine flour and salt. Add the yeast mixture and olive oil. Mix until a dough forms.

- Turn the dough onto a floured surface and knead for about 8-10 minutes until smooth and elastic.
3. **First Rise:**
    - Place the dough in a lightly oiled bowl, cover, and let rise in a warm place for 1-1½ hours, or until doubled in size.
4. **Shape and Fill the Bread:**
    - Punch down the dough and divide it into two equal pieces.
    - Roll each piece into a rectangle on a floured surface.
    - Spread a generous layer of Matbucha over one of the rectangles, leaving a small border around the edges.
    - Roll the dough up tightly from one end to the other, like a jelly roll.
    - Place the rolled dough seam-side down on a greased or parchment-lined baking sheet. Repeat with the second piece of dough.
5. **Second Rise:**
    - Cover the loaves and let rise for 30-45 minutes, or until puffy.
6. **Preheat Oven:**
    - Preheat your oven to 375°F (190°C).
7. **Bake:**
    - Bake the loaves for 25-30 minutes, or until they are golden brown and sound hollow when tapped on the bottom.
8. **Cool:**
    - Let the bread cool on a wire rack before slicing.

Matbucha Bread is aromatic and flavorful, perfect for serving alongside dips, soups, or simply enjoying on its own. The Matbucha filling adds a delightful twist to a classic bread recipe. Enjoy!

Khubz

Ingredients:

- 3 cups all-purpose flour
- 1 packet (2¼ tsp) active dry yeast
- 1½ cups warm water (110°F or 45°C)
- 1 tbsp granulated sugar
- 1½ tsp salt
- 2 tbsp olive oil

Instructions:

1. **Activate the Yeast:**
   - In a small bowl, dissolve the sugar in warm water. Sprinkle the yeast over the top and let it sit for 5-10 minutes until it becomes frothy.
2. **Mix the Dough:**
   - In a large bowl, combine the flour and salt.
   - Add the yeast mixture and olive oil. Mix until the dough starts to come together.
3. **Knead:**
   - Turn the dough out onto a floured surface and knead for about 8-10 minutes, until the dough is smooth and elastic.
4. **First Rise:**
   - Place the dough in a lightly oiled bowl, cover it with plastic wrap or a damp cloth, and let it rise in a warm place for about 1 hour, or until doubled in size.
5. **Shape the Khubz:**
   - Punch down the dough and turn it onto a floured surface. Divide the dough into 8-10 equal pieces.
   - Roll each piece into a ball and then flatten it with a rolling pin into a circle about ¼-inch thick.
6. **Preheat Oven:**
   - Preheat your oven to 475°F (245°C). If using a pizza stone, place it in the oven to preheat as well.
7. **Bake:**
   - Place the rolled-out dough circles onto a baking sheet or preheated pizza stone.
   - Bake for 2-3 minutes, or until the bread puffs up and is lightly golden. The bread should form a pocket as it bakes.
8. **Cool:**
   - Remove the Khubz from the oven and let it cool on a wire rack.

Khubz is perfect for making sandwiches, scooping up dips like hummus, or serving with various Middle Eastern dishes. Enjoy this soft and versatile flatbread fresh from the oven!

Tachina Bread

Ingredients:

For the Dough:

- 3½ cups all-purpose flour
- 1 packet (2¼ tsp) active dry yeast
- 1½ cups warm water (110°F or 45°C)
- ¼ cup tahini (pure sesame paste)
- 2 tbsp olive oil
- 1 tbsp sugar
- 1½ tsp salt

For the Topping (optional):

- Sesame seeds
- Coarse sea salt

Instructions:

1. **Activate the Yeast:**
    - In a small bowl, dissolve the sugar in warm water. Sprinkle the yeast over the top and let it sit for 5-10 minutes until frothy.
2. **Mix the Dough:**
    - In a large bowl, combine flour and salt.
    - Add the yeast mixture, tahini, and olive oil. Mix until the dough starts to come together.
3. **Knead:**
    - Turn the dough onto a floured surface and knead for about 8-10 minutes, until smooth and elastic.
4. **First Rise:**
    - Place the dough in a lightly oiled bowl, cover with plastic wrap or a damp cloth, and let it rise in a warm place for about 1 hour, or until doubled in size.
5. **Shape the Bread:**
    - Punch down the dough and turn it out onto a floured surface. Shape the dough into a loaf or divide it into smaller pieces to make rolls.
    - Place the shaped dough on a greased or parchment-lined baking sheet.
6. **Second Rise:**
    - Cover the dough with a damp cloth or plastic wrap and let it rise for another 30-45 minutes, or until puffy.
7. **Preheat Oven:**
    - Preheat your oven to 375°F (190°C).

8. **Prepare for Baking:**
    - If desired, brush the top of the dough with a little water or olive oil and sprinkle with sesame seeds and/or coarse sea salt.
9. **Bake:**
    - Bake for 25-30 minutes (for a loaf) or 15-20 minutes (for rolls), or until the bread is golden brown and sounds hollow when tapped on the bottom.
10. **Cool:**
    - Let the bread cool on a wire rack before slicing.

Serving Suggestions:

- Tachina Bread is excellent for sandwiches, or served with dips such as hummus or baba ganoush.
- Enjoy it with a bit of butter or olive oil for a simple and satisfying snack.

This bread's nutty flavor and soft texture make it a wonderful addition to any meal. Enjoy!

Zaatar Bread

Ingredients:

For the Dough:

- 3½ cups all-purpose flour
- 1 packet (2¼ tsp) active dry yeast
- 1½ cups warm water (110°F or 45°C)
- ¼ cup olive oil
- 1 tbsp sugar
- 1½ tsp salt

For the Za'atar Topping:

- ¼ cup olive oil
- 3 tbsp za'atar spice blend (store-bought or homemade)
- 1-2 cloves garlic, minced (optional)
- 1 tbsp sesame seeds (optional)

Za'atar Spice Blend (if making your own):

- 2 tbsp dried thyme
- 1 tbsp dried oregano
- 1 tbsp sumac
- 1 tbsp sesame seeds
- 1 tsp salt

Instructions:

1. **Prepare the Za'atar Spice Blend (if making your own):**
   - Mix dried thyme, oregano, sumac, sesame seeds, and salt in a small bowl. Set aside.
2. **Activate the Yeast:**
   - In a small bowl, dissolve sugar in warm water. Sprinkle yeast over and let sit for 5-10 minutes until frothy.
3. **Mix the Dough:**
   - In a large bowl, combine flour and salt.
   - Add the yeast mixture and olive oil. Mix until a dough forms.
4. **Knead:**
   - Turn the dough onto a floured surface and knead for about 8-10 minutes, until smooth and elastic.
5. **First Rise:**

- Place the dough in a lightly oiled bowl, cover, and let rise in a warm place for about 1 hour, or until doubled in size.

6. **Shape and Prepare for Topping:**
   - Punch down the dough and turn it out onto a floured surface. Divide it into two equal pieces.
   - Roll each piece into a flat oval or round shape, about ½-inch thick.
   - Transfer the shaped dough to a baking sheet lined with parchment paper.

7. **Prepare the Topping:**
   - Mix olive oil with minced garlic (if using) in a small bowl.
   - Brush the olive oil mixture generously over the dough.
   - Sprinkle za'atar spice blend evenly over the top. Add sesame seeds if desired.

8. **Second Rise:**
   - Cover the dough lightly with a cloth and let it rise for another 30 minutes.

9. **Preheat Oven:**
   - Preheat your oven to 375°F (190°C).

10. **Bake:**
    - Bake for 20-25 minutes, or until the bread is golden brown and sounds hollow when tapped.

11. **Cool:**
    - Let the bread cool slightly on a wire rack before slicing.

Za'atar Bread is perfect for serving with dips, as a sandwich base, or simply enjoyed on its own. Enjoy the aromatic and savory flavors of this Middle Eastern classic!

Sabich Sandwich Bread

Ingredients:

For the Dough:

- 3½ cups all-purpose flour
- 1 packet (2¼ tsp) active dry yeast
- 1½ cups warm water (110°F or 45°C)
- ¼ cup olive oil
- 1 tbsp sugar
- 1½ tsp salt

For Assembly:

- 1 egg (for brushing, optional)
- Sesame seeds (optional)

Instructions:

1. **Activate the Yeast:**
    - In a small bowl, dissolve sugar in warm water. Sprinkle yeast over the top and let it sit for 5-10 minutes until frothy.
2. **Mix the Dough:**
    - In a large bowl, combine flour and salt.
    - Add the yeast mixture and olive oil. Mix until a dough forms.
3. **Knead:**
    - Turn the dough onto a floured surface and knead for about 8-10 minutes until smooth and elastic.
4. **First Rise:**
    - Place the dough in a lightly oiled bowl, cover with plastic wrap or a damp cloth, and let it rise in a warm place for about 1 hour, or until doubled in size.
5. **Shape the Bread:**
    - Punch down the dough and turn it onto a floured surface. Shape into a loaf or divide into smaller pieces for rolls.
    - Place the shaped dough into a greased loaf pan or on a baking sheet.
6. **Second Rise:**
    - Cover the dough and let it rise for another 30 minutes, or until puffy.
7. **Preheat Oven:**
    - Preheat your oven to 375°F (190°C).
8. **Prepare for Baking:**
    - Brush the top of the loaf with beaten egg if using, and sprinkle with sesame seeds if desired.

9. **Bake:**
    - Bake for 25-30 minutes, or until the bread is golden brown and sounds hollow when tapped.
10. **Cool:**
    - Let the bread cool on a wire rack before slicing.

Serving Suggestions:

- Slice the bread and use it to make a Sabich sandwich, layering with fried eggplant, hard-boiled eggs, hummus, tahini, salad, and pickles.

This soft, slightly chewy bread is perfect for holding all the delicious fillings of a Sabich sandwich. Enjoy!

Rye Bread

Ingredients:

For the Dough:

- 1½ cups warm water (110°F or 45°C)
- 1 packet (2¼ tsp) active dry yeast
- 2 tbsp molasses
- 2 tbsp vegetable oil
- 1¼ cups rye flour
- 2¼ cups all-purpose flour
- 1 tbsp caraway seeds (optional)
- 1½ tsp salt

For the Topping (optional):

- Caraway seeds
- Coarse sea salt

Instructions:

1. **Activate the Yeast:**
    - In a small bowl, dissolve molasses in warm water. Sprinkle yeast over and let sit for 5-10 minutes until frothy.
2. **Mix the Dough:**
    - In a large bowl, combine rye flour, all-purpose flour, salt, and caraway seeds (if using).
    - Add the yeast mixture and vegetable oil. Mix until a dough forms.
3. **Knead:**
    - Turn the dough onto a floured surface and knead for about 8-10 minutes until smooth and elastic.
4. **First Rise:**
    - Place the dough in a lightly oiled bowl, cover with plastic wrap or a damp cloth, and let it rise in a warm place for about 1-1½ hours, or until doubled in size.
5. **Shape the Loaf:**
    - Punch down the dough and turn it onto a floured surface. Shape it into a loaf or place it in a greased loaf pan.
6. **Second Rise:**
    - Cover the dough and let it rise for another 30-45 minutes, or until puffy.
7. **Preheat Oven:**
    - Preheat your oven to 375°F (190°C).
8. **Prepare for Baking:**

- Brush the top of the loaf with water and sprinkle with additional caraway seeds and/or coarse sea salt if desired.
9. **Bake:**
    - Bake for 30-35 minutes, or until the bread is golden brown and sounds hollow when tapped.
10. **Cool:**
    - Let the bread cool on a wire rack before slicing.

Rye Bread is perfect for sandwiches, toast, or with hearty soups. Enjoy the robust flavor and satisfying texture of this classic bread!

Israeli Focaccia

Ingredients:

For the Dough:

- 3½ cups all-purpose flour
- 1 packet (2¼ tsp) active dry yeast
- 1½ cups warm water (110°F or 45°C)
- ¼ cup olive oil, plus extra for drizzling
- 1 tbsp sugar
- 1½ tsp salt

For the Topping:

- 2 tbsp olive oil
- 2-3 cloves garlic, thinly sliced
- 1 tbsp fresh rosemary, chopped (or thyme)
- 1 tsp coarse sea salt
- 1 tsp za'atar spice blend (optional)

Instructions:

1. **Activate the Yeast:**
   - In a small bowl, dissolve sugar in warm water. Sprinkle yeast over and let it sit for 5-10 minutes until frothy.
2. **Mix the Dough:**
   - In a large bowl, combine flour and salt.
   - Add the yeast mixture and ¼ cup olive oil. Mix until a dough forms.
3. **Knead:**
   - Turn the dough onto a floured surface and knead for about 8-10 minutes until smooth and elastic.
4. **First Rise:**
   - Place the dough in a lightly oiled bowl, cover with plastic wrap or a damp cloth, and let it rise in a warm place for about 1-1½ hours, or until doubled in size.
5. **Prepare the Topping:**
   - While the dough rises, mix olive oil with garlic slices. Set aside.
6. **Shape and Second Rise:**
   - Punch down the dough and turn it onto a floured surface. Stretch it out into a rectangle or circle, about 1-inch thick.
   - Transfer the dough to a greased or parchment-lined baking sheet.
   - Use your fingers to dimple the dough all over.
7. **Add Toppings:**

- Brush the dough with the garlic-infused olive oil.
- Sprinkle with rosemary, sea salt, and za'atar spice blend if using.
8. **Preheat Oven:**
    - Preheat your oven to 425°F (220°C).
9. **Bake:**
    - Bake for 20-25 minutes, or until the focaccia is golden brown and sounds hollow when tapped.
10. **Cool:**
    - Let the focaccia cool slightly before slicing.

Israeli Focaccia is great served warm or at room temperature, perfect as an appetizer, side dish, or with a spread of olive oil and balsamic vinegar. Enjoy the fragrant herbs and crispy crust!

Pita with Hummus

Ingredients:

For the Pita Bread:

- 3 cups all-purpose flour
- 1 packet (2¼ tsp) active dry yeast
- 1½ cups warm water (110°F or 45°C)
- 1 tbsp olive oil
- 1 tbsp sugar
- 1½ tsp salt

For the Hummus:

- 1 can (15 oz) chickpeas, drained and rinsed
- ¼ cup tahini (sesame paste)
- 2-3 cloves garlic, minced
- ¼ cup lemon juice
- 2 tbsp olive oil
- 1 tsp ground cumin
- Salt to taste
- Water (as needed for consistency)

Instructions:

1. Make the Pita Bread:

- **Activate the Yeast:** Dissolve sugar in warm water. Sprinkle yeast over and let sit for 5-10 minutes until frothy.
- **Mix the Dough:** In a large bowl, combine flour and salt. Add yeast mixture and olive oil. Mix until dough forms.
- **Knead:** Turn onto a floured surface and knead for 8-10 minutes until smooth.
- **First Rise:** Place in a lightly oiled bowl, cover, and let rise for 1 hour, until doubled.
- **Shape and Second Rise:** Punch down, divide into 8 pieces, and roll into circles. Let rise for 30 minutes.
- **Bake:** Preheat oven to 475°F (245°C). Bake circles for 2-3 minutes on a baking sheet or pizza stone until they puff up.

2. Make the Hummus:

- **Blend Ingredients:** In a food processor, combine chickpeas, tahini, garlic, lemon juice, olive oil, cumin, and salt. Blend until smooth, adding water as needed to reach desired consistency.

3. Serve:

- **Enjoy:** Cut the warm pita into wedges and serve with hummus for dipping.

This combination is perfect for a quick snack or a light meal. Enjoy the soft, fluffy pita with the creamy, flavorful hummus!

Flatbread

Ingredients:

- 2 cups all-purpose flour
- 1 tsp salt
- 1 tsp baking powder
- 2 tbsp olive oil
- ¾ cup warm water (adjust as needed)

Instructions:

1. **Mix the Dough:**
    - In a large bowl, combine flour, salt, and baking powder.
    - Add olive oil and gradually mix in warm water until a dough forms. The dough should be soft but not sticky.
2. **Knead:**
    - Turn the dough onto a floured surface and knead for 2-3 minutes until smooth.
3. **Rest:**
    - Cover the dough with a damp cloth and let it rest for 15 minutes.
4. **Shape the Flatbreads:**
    - Divide the dough into 6-8 equal pieces.
    - Roll each piece into a thin circle or oval, about ¼-inch thick.
5. **Cook:**
    - Heat a skillet or griddle over medium-high heat. Cook each flatbread for 1-2 minutes per side, or until brown spots appear and the bread is cooked through.
6. **Serve:**
    - Enjoy warm or at room temperature with your favorite dips, or use as a wrap or sandwich base.

This flatbread is easy to make and adaptable to various flavors by adding herbs or spices to the dough. Enjoy!

Cheese Bourekas

Ingredients:

For the Dough:

- 1 package (17.3 oz) frozen puff pastry sheets (2 sheets), thawed
- 1 egg, beaten (for egg wash)

For the Cheese Filling:

- 1 cup ricotta cheese
- 1 cup feta cheese, crumbled
- 1 cup shredded mozzarella cheese
- 1 egg
- 2 tbsp fresh parsley, chopped (or dill)
- 1 tsp dried oregano
- Salt and pepper to taste

Instructions:

1. **Prepare the Cheese Filling:**
    - In a mixing bowl, combine ricotta cheese, feta cheese, mozzarella cheese, egg, parsley, oregano, salt, and pepper. Mix until well combined.
2. **Prepare the Puff Pastry:**
    - Preheat your oven to 375°F (190°C).
    - On a lightly floured surface, roll out each puff pastry sheet. Cut each sheet into squares or rectangles, about 4x4 inches in size.
3. **Fill and Shape the Bourekas:**
    - Place a spoonful of the cheese filling in the center of each pastry square.
    - Fold the pastry over the filling to form a triangle or rectangle, sealing the edges by pressing with a fork or pinching with your fingers.
4. **Apply Egg Wash:**
    - Place the filled bourekas on a baking sheet lined with parchment paper.
    - Brush the tops of the bourekas with the beaten egg to give them a golden, glossy finish. You can also sprinkle sesame seeds on top if desired.
5. **Bake:**
    - Bake for 20-25 minutes, or until the bourekas are golden brown and puffed up.
6. **Cool:**
    - Allow the bourekas to cool slightly before serving.

Serving Suggestions:

- Serve warm or at room temperature.
- These bourekas are great with a side of salad or as part of a mezze platter.

Enjoy your homemade Cheese Bourekas! They're perfect for a delicious snack or a special treat.

Spinach Bourekas

Ingredients:

For the Dough:

- 1 package (17.3 oz) frozen puff pastry sheets (2 sheets), thawed
- 1 egg, beaten (for egg wash)

For the Spinach Filling:

- 2 cups fresh spinach, chopped (or 1 cup frozen spinach, thawed and squeezed dry)
- 1 cup ricotta cheese
- ½ cup feta cheese, crumbled
- 1 egg
- 2 tbsp fresh dill or parsley, chopped
- 1 small onion, finely chopped
- 2 cloves garlic, minced
- 1 tbsp olive oil
- Salt and pepper to taste

Instructions:

1. **Prepare the Spinach Filling:**
    - Heat olive oil in a pan over medium heat. Sauté the onion and garlic until softened.
    - Add the spinach and cook until wilted and any excess moisture is evaporated. Let cool slightly.
    - In a bowl, combine the spinach mixture with ricotta cheese, feta cheese, egg, dill or parsley, salt, and pepper. Mix well.
2. **Prepare the Puff Pastry:**
    - Preheat your oven to 375°F (190°C).
    - On a lightly floured surface, roll out each puff pastry sheet. Cut into squares or rectangles, about 4x4 inches in size.
3. **Fill and Shape the Bourekas:**
    - Place a spoonful of the spinach filling in the center of each pastry square.
    - Fold the pastry over the filling to form a triangle or rectangle, sealing the edges by pressing with a fork or pinching with your fingers.
4. **Apply Egg Wash:**
    - Place the filled bourekas on a baking sheet lined with parchment paper.
    - Brush the tops of the bourekas with the beaten egg to give them a golden, glossy finish.
5. **Bake:**

- - Bake for 20-25 minutes, or until the bourekas are golden brown and puffed up.
6. **Cool:**
   - Allow the bourekas to cool slightly before serving.

Serving Suggestions:

- Serve warm or at room temperature.
- Enjoy as a snack, appetizer, or part of a mezze platter.

These Spinach Bourekas are crispy, flavorful, and a great way to enjoy a delicious combination of spinach and cheese!

Sweet Challah

Ingredients:

For the Dough:

- 1 cup warm water (110°F or 45°C)
- 1 packet (2¼ tsp) active dry yeast
- ¼ cup granulated sugar
- ¼ cup honey
- ¼ cup vegetable oil
- 4 large eggs
- 4½ cups all-purpose flour
- 1½ tsp salt

For the Egg Wash:

- 1 egg, beaten
- 1 tbsp water

For the Topping (optional):

- Sesame seeds
- Poppy seeds

Instructions:

1. **Activate the Yeast:**
   - In a small bowl, combine warm water and sugar. Sprinkle yeast over the top and let sit for 5-10 minutes until frothy.
2. **Mix the Dough:**
   - In a large bowl, whisk together the honey, vegetable oil, and eggs.
   - Add the yeast mixture and mix well.
   - Gradually add flour and salt, mixing until the dough begins to come together.
3. **Knead:**
   - Turn the dough onto a floured surface and knead for about 8-10 minutes, until smooth and elastic.
4. **First Rise:**
   - Place the dough in a lightly oiled bowl, cover with plastic wrap or a damp cloth, and let it rise in a warm place for about 1½ hours, or until doubled in size.
5. **Shape the Challah:**
   - Punch down the dough and turn it onto a floured surface. Divide the dough into three equal pieces.

- Roll each piece into a long strand, about 14 inches long.
- Braid the three strands together, pinching the ends to seal. Place the braided loaf on a parchment-lined baking sheet.

6. **Second Rise:**
   - Cover the braided loaf with a damp cloth and let it rise for another 30-45 minutes, or until puffy.
7. **Preheat Oven:**
   - Preheat your oven to 375°F (190°C).
8. **Prepare for Baking:**
   - In a small bowl, mix the beaten egg with 1 tbsp water. Brush this egg wash over the braided loaf.
   - Sprinkle with sesame seeds or poppy seeds if desired.
9. **Bake:**
   - Bake for 25-30 minutes, or until the challah is golden brown and sounds hollow when tapped on the bottom.
10. **Cool:**
    - Let the challah cool on a wire rack before slicing.

Serving Suggestions:

- Enjoy as is, or with a spread of butter, honey, or jam.
- Perfect for breakfast, brunch, or as a special treat.

Sweet Challah is a beautiful and delicious bread that's great for family gatherings, holidays, or any day you want to add a touch of sweetness to your meal. Enjoy!

Oregano Bread

Ingredients:

For the Dough:

- 3½ cups all-purpose flour
- 1 packet (2¼ tsp) active dry yeast
- 1½ cups warm water (110°F or 45°C)
- ¼ cup olive oil
- 2 tbsp fresh oregano leaves (or 2 tsp dried oregano)
- 1 tbsp sugar
- 1½ tsp salt

For the Topping (optional):

- 2 tbsp olive oil
- 1 tbsp fresh oregano leaves or dried oregano
- Coarse sea salt

Instructions:

1. **Activate the Yeast:**
   - In a small bowl, dissolve sugar in warm water. Sprinkle yeast over and let it sit for 5-10 minutes until frothy.
2. **Mix the Dough:**
   - In a large bowl, combine flour, salt, and oregano.
   - Add the yeast mixture and olive oil. Mix until a dough forms.
3. **Knead:**
   - Turn the dough onto a floured surface and knead for about 8-10 minutes, until smooth and elastic.
4. **First Rise:**
   - Place the dough in a lightly oiled bowl, cover with plastic wrap or a damp cloth, and let it rise in a warm place for about 1 hour, or until doubled in size.
5. **Shape the Bread:**
   - Punch down the dough and turn it onto a floured surface. Shape into a loaf or divide into smaller pieces if you prefer rolls.
   - Place the shaped dough on a baking sheet lined with parchment paper or in a greased loaf pan.
6. **Second Rise:**
   - Cover the dough and let it rise for another 30 minutes, or until puffy.
7. **Preheat Oven:**
   - Preheat your oven to 375°F (190°C).

8. **Prepare for Baking:**
    - Brush the top of the loaf with olive oil.
    - Sprinkle with additional oregano and coarse sea salt if desired.
9. **Bake:**
    - Bake for 25-30 minutes, or until the bread is golden brown and sounds hollow when tapped.
10. **Cool:**
    - Allow the bread to cool on a wire rack before slicing.

Serving Suggestions:

- Serve warm with olive oil for dipping.
- Use as a flavorful accompaniment to soups, salads, or pasta dishes.

This Oregano Bread is aromatic and savory, with a delightful herbaceous flavor that enhances any meal. Enjoy!

Onion Bread

Ingredients:

For the Dough:

- 3½ cups all-purpose flour
- 1 packet (2¼ tsp) active dry yeast
- 1½ cups warm water (110°F or 45°C)
- ¼ cup olive oil
- 1 tbsp sugar
- 1½ tsp salt

For the Caramelized Onions:

- 2 large onions, thinly sliced
- 2 tbsp olive oil
- 1 tsp sugar (optional, for extra caramelization)
- Salt and pepper to taste

For the Topping (optional):

- 1 egg, beaten (for egg wash)
- 1 tbsp fresh thyme or rosemary, chopped (optional)

Instructions:

1. **Caramelize the Onions:**
    - Heat olive oil in a skillet over medium heat.
    - Add onions, and cook slowly, stirring occasionally, until they are golden brown and caramelized, about 15-20 minutes. Add sugar during cooking if desired. Season with salt and pepper. Let cool.
2. **Activate the Yeast:**
    - In a small bowl, dissolve sugar in warm water. Sprinkle yeast over and let sit for 5-10 minutes until frothy.
3. **Mix the Dough:**
    - In a large bowl, combine flour and salt.
    - Add the yeast mixture and olive oil. Mix until a dough forms.
4. **Knead:**
    - Turn the dough onto a floured surface and knead for about 8-10 minutes until smooth and elastic.
5. **First Rise:**

- Place the dough in a lightly oiled bowl, cover with plastic wrap or a damp cloth, and let it rise in a warm place for about 1 hour, or until doubled in size.
6. **Incorporate Onions:**
    - Punch down the dough and turn it onto a floured surface. Flatten slightly and spread the caramelized onions over the dough.
    - Fold the dough to incorporate the onions, kneading lightly to distribute them evenly.
7. **Shape and Second Rise:**
    - Shape the dough into a loaf and place it in a greased loaf pan or on a baking sheet.
    - Cover and let it rise for another 30 minutes, or until puffy.
8. **Preheat Oven:**
    - Preheat your oven to 375°F (190°C).
9. **Prepare for Baking:**
    - Brush the top of the loaf with beaten egg if using. Sprinkle with fresh thyme or rosemary if desired.
10. **Bake:**
    - Bake for 30-35 minutes, or until the bread is golden brown and sounds hollow when tapped.
11. **Cool:**
    - Let the bread cool on a wire rack before slicing.

Serving Suggestions:

- Enjoy warm with butter or as a sandwich bread.
- Pairs well with soups, salads, or as an accompaniment to cheese.

Onion Bread is flavorful and aromatic, with a delightful combination of soft, tender crumb and sweet, caramelized onions. Enjoy!

Barley Bread

Ingredients:

For the Dough:

- 1 cup barley flour
- 2 cups all-purpose flour
- 1 packet (2¼ tsp) active dry yeast
- 1½ cups warm water (110°F or 45°C)
- 2 tbsp honey or molasses
- 2 tbsp olive oil
- 1½ tsp salt

For the Topping (optional):

- 1 egg, beaten (for egg wash)
- 1 tbsp rolled oats or barley flakes (optional)

Instructions:

1. **Activate the Yeast:**
   - In a small bowl, dissolve honey or molasses in warm water. Sprinkle yeast over and let it sit for 5-10 minutes until frothy.
2. **Mix the Dough:**
   - In a large bowl, combine barley flour, all-purpose flour, and salt.
   - Add the yeast mixture and olive oil. Mix until a dough forms.
3. **Knead:**
   - Turn the dough onto a floured surface and knead for about 8-10 minutes until smooth and elastic.
4. **First Rise:**
   - Place the dough in a lightly oiled bowl, cover with plastic wrap or a damp cloth, and let it rise in a warm place for about 1 hour, or until doubled in size.
5. **Shape the Bread:**
   - Punch down the dough and turn it onto a floured surface. Shape into a loaf or divide into smaller pieces if you prefer rolls.
   - Place the shaped dough on a baking sheet lined with parchment paper or in a greased loaf pan.
6. **Second Rise:**
   - Cover the dough and let it rise for another 30-45 minutes, or until puffy.
7. **Preheat Oven:**
   - Preheat your oven to 375°F (190°C).
8. **Prepare for Baking:**

- Brush the top of the loaf with beaten egg if using. Sprinkle with rolled oats or barley flakes if desired.
9. **Bake:**
    - Bake for 30-35 minutes, or until the bread is golden brown and sounds hollow when tapped.
10. **Cool:**
    - Allow the bread to cool on a wire rack before slicing.

Serving Suggestions:

- Enjoy with butter, cheese, or as a base for sandwiches.
- Pairs well with soups, stews, or salads.

Barley Bread has a slightly nutty flavor and a hearty texture, making it a great choice for a wholesome and satisfying bread. Enjoy!

Herb Flatbread

Ingredients:

For the Dough:

- 2 cups all-purpose flour
- 1 packet (2¼ tsp) active dry yeast
- 1 cup warm water (110°F or 45°C)
- 2 tbsp olive oil
- 1 tsp sugar
- 1 tsp salt
- 2 tbsp fresh herbs (such as rosemary, thyme, or parsley), finely chopped, or 2 tsp dried herbs

For the Topping:

- 2 tbsp olive oil
- 1 tbsp fresh herbs (such as rosemary or thyme), chopped, or 1 tsp dried herbs
- Coarse sea salt

Instructions:

1. **Activate the Yeast:**
    - In a small bowl, dissolve sugar in warm water. Sprinkle yeast over and let it sit for 5-10 minutes until frothy.
2. **Mix the Dough:**
    - In a large bowl, combine flour, salt, and your choice of fresh or dried herbs.
    - Add the yeast mixture and olive oil. Mix until a dough forms.
3. **Knead:**
    - Turn the dough onto a floured surface and knead for about 5-7 minutes until smooth and elastic.
4. **First Rise:**
    - Place the dough in a lightly oiled bowl, cover with plastic wrap or a damp cloth, and let it rise in a warm place for about 1 hour, or until doubled in size.
5. **Prepare for Shaping:**
    - Punch down the dough and turn it onto a floured surface. Divide the dough into 2-4 pieces, depending on the size of flatbreads you prefer.
    - Roll each piece into a thin, flat circle or rectangle, about ¼ inch thick.
6. **Preheat Oven:**
    - Preheat your oven to 475°F (245°C). If using a pizza stone, place it in the oven to preheat as well.
7. **Prepare the Flatbreads:**

- Place the rolled-out dough onto a parchment-lined baking sheet or a preheated pizza stone.
    - Brush the tops with olive oil and sprinkle with additional fresh or dried herbs and coarse sea salt.
8. **Bake:**
    - Bake for 8-10 minutes, or until the flatbreads are golden brown and crispy.
9. **Cool:**
    - Allow the flatbreads to cool slightly before slicing or serving.

Serving Suggestions:

- Serve with hummus, tzatziki, or a variety of dips.
- Use as a base for appetizers, like mini flatbread pizzas, or as a side with soups and salads.

Herb Flatbread is fragrant with fresh herbs and has a delightful crispiness, making it a versatile addition to any meal or gathering. Enjoy!

Sesame Bagels

Ingredients:

For the Bagels:

- 4 cups bread flour
- 1 packet (2¼ tsp) active dry yeast
- 1½ cups warm water (110°F or 45°C)
- 2 tbsp sugar
- 1½ tsp salt
- 1 tbsp vegetable oil

For Boiling and Topping:

- 2 tbsp honey (for boiling water)
- 1 cup sesame seeds
- 1 egg, beaten (for egg wash)

Instructions:

1. **Activate the Yeast:**
   - In a small bowl, dissolve sugar in warm water. Sprinkle yeast over and let it sit for 5-10 minutes until frothy.
2. **Mix the Dough:**
   - In a large bowl, combine bread flour and salt.
   - Add the yeast mixture and vegetable oil. Mix until a dough forms.
3. **Knead:**
   - Turn the dough onto a floured surface and knead for about 10 minutes until smooth and elastic.
4. **First Rise:**
   - Place the dough in a lightly oiled bowl, cover with plastic wrap or a damp cloth, and let it rise in a warm place for about 1 hour, or until doubled in size.
5. **Shape the Bagels:**
   - Punch down the dough and turn it onto a floured surface. Divide into 8-10 pieces.
   - Shape each piece into a ball and then use your thumb to make a hole in the center. Stretch the hole to form a bagel shape.
6. **Prepare for Boiling:**
   - Bring a large pot of water to a boil and add honey.
   - Gently place bagels in the boiling water (3-4 at a time) for 1-2 minutes per side.
7. **Prepare for Baking:**
   - Preheat your oven to 425°F (220°C).
   - Remove bagels from water and drain. Place on a parchment-lined baking sheet.

- Brush the tops with beaten egg and sprinkle with sesame seeds.
8. **Bake:**
    - Bake for 20-25 minutes, or until bagels are golden brown and sound hollow when tapped.
9. **Cool:**
    - Let the bagels cool on a wire rack before slicing.

Serving Suggestions:

- Serve with cream cheese, lox, or your favorite bagel toppings.
- Great for breakfast or brunch.

Sesame Bagels are chewy with a delicious sesame seed crunch, perfect for a classic bagel experience. Enjoy!

Fennel Seed Bread

Ingredients:

For the Dough:

- 3½ cups all-purpose flour
- 1 packet (2¼ tsp) active dry yeast
- 1½ cups warm water (110°F or 45°C)
- 2 tbsp sugar
- 2 tbsp olive oil
- 1½ tsp salt
- 2 tbsp fennel seeds

For the Topping (optional):

- 1 egg, beaten (for egg wash)
- 1 tbsp fennel seeds (for sprinkling)

Instructions:

1. **Activate the Yeast:**
   - In a small bowl, dissolve sugar in warm water. Sprinkle yeast over and let it sit for 5-10 minutes until frothy.
2. **Mix the Dough:**
   - In a large bowl, combine flour, salt, and fennel seeds.
   - Add the yeast mixture and olive oil. Mix until a dough forms.
3. **Knead:**
   - Turn the dough onto a floured surface and knead for about 8-10 minutes, until smooth and elastic.
4. **First Rise:**
   - Place the dough in a lightly oiled bowl, cover with plastic wrap or a damp cloth, and let it rise in a warm place for about 1 hour, or until doubled in size.
5. **Shape the Bread:**
   - Punch down the dough and turn it onto a floured surface. Shape into a loaf or divide into smaller pieces if you prefer rolls.
   - Place the shaped dough on a parchment-lined baking sheet or in a greased loaf pan.
6. **Second Rise:**
   - Cover the dough and let it rise for another 30-45 minutes, or until puffy.
7. **Preheat Oven:**
   - Preheat your oven to 375°F (190°C).
8. **Prepare for Baking:**

- Brush the top of the loaf with beaten egg if using. Sprinkle with additional fennel seeds.
9. **Bake:**
   - Bake for 25-30 minutes, or until the bread is golden brown and sounds hollow when tapped.
10. **Cool:**
    - Allow the bread to cool on a wire rack before slicing.

Serving Suggestions:

- Enjoy as is or with a bit of butter.
- Pairs well with cheeses, charcuterie, or as a side for soups and salads.

Fennel Seed Bread has a distinctive flavor and aroma that pairs beautifully with a variety of dishes. The fennel seeds provide a pleasant crunch and a subtle licorice-like taste. Enjoy baking and savoring your homemade bread!

Tomato Bread

Ingredients:

For the Dough:

- 3½ cups all-purpose flour
- 1 packet (2¼ tsp) active dry yeast
- 1 cup warm water (110°F or 45°C)
- ¼ cup tomato paste
- 2 tbsp olive oil
- 2 tbsp sugar
- 1½ tsp salt
- 1 tsp dried oregano (optional)

For the Topping (optional):

- 1 tbsp olive oil
- 1 tsp dried oregano or fresh basil, chopped

Instructions:

1. **Activate the Yeast:**
    - In a small bowl, dissolve sugar in warm water. Sprinkle yeast over and let it sit for 5-10 minutes until frothy.
2. **Mix the Dough:**
    - In a large bowl, combine flour, salt, and dried oregano if using.
    - Add the yeast mixture, tomato paste, and olive oil. Mix until a dough forms.
3. **Knead:**
    - Turn the dough onto a floured surface and knead for about 8-10 minutes, until smooth and elastic.
4. **First Rise:**
    - Place the dough in a lightly oiled bowl, cover with plastic wrap or a damp cloth, and let it rise in a warm place for about 1 hour, or until doubled in size.
5. **Shape the Bread:**
    - Punch down the dough and turn it onto a floured surface. Shape into a loaf or divide into rolls if preferred.
    - Place the shaped dough on a parchment-lined baking sheet or in a greased loaf pan.
6. **Second Rise:**
    - Cover and let the dough rise for another 30-45 minutes, or until puffy.
7. **Preheat Oven:**
    - Preheat your oven to 375°F (190°C).

8. **Prepare for Baking:**
   - Brush the top of the loaf with olive oil and sprinkle with additional oregano or basil if desired.
9. **Bake:**
   - Bake for 30-35 minutes, or until the bread is golden brown and sounds hollow when tapped.
10. **Cool:**
    - Allow the bread to cool on a wire rack before slicing.

Serving Suggestions:

- Serve with a bit of butter or olive oil.
- Pairs well with soups, salads, or as a side for Italian dishes.

Tomato Bread has a wonderful, tangy flavor with a soft, moist crumb. It's a great addition to many meals and a delicious twist on traditional bread. Enjoy!

Green Olive Bread

Ingredients:

For the Dough:

- 3½ cups all-purpose flour
- 1 packet (2¼ tsp) active dry yeast
- 1½ cups warm water (110°F or 45°C)
- 2 tbsp olive oil
- 2 tbsp sugar
- 1½ tsp salt
- 1 cup green olives, pitted and chopped

For the Topping (optional):

- 1 egg, beaten (for egg wash)
- 2 tbsp chopped fresh rosemary or thyme (optional)

Instructions:

1. **Activate the Yeast:**
   - In a small bowl, dissolve sugar in warm water. Sprinkle yeast over and let it sit for 5-10 minutes until frothy.
2. **Mix the Dough:**
   - In a large bowl, combine flour and salt.
   - Add the yeast mixture and olive oil. Mix until a dough forms.
3. **Incorporate the Olives:**
   - Turn the dough onto a floured surface and knead for about 5 minutes.
   - Gently knead in the chopped green olives until evenly distributed.
4. **Knead:**
   - Continue kneading the dough for about 8-10 minutes, until smooth and elastic.
5. **First Rise:**
   - Place the dough in a lightly oiled bowl, cover with plastic wrap or a damp cloth, and let it rise in a warm place for about 1 hour, or until doubled in size.
6. **Shape the Bread:**
   - Punch down the dough and turn it onto a floured surface. Shape into a loaf or divide into smaller pieces if making rolls.
   - Place the shaped dough on a parchment-lined baking sheet or in a greased loaf pan.
7. **Second Rise:**
   - Cover the dough and let it rise for another 30-45 minutes, or until puffy.
8. **Preheat Oven:**

- Preheat your oven to 375°F (190°C).
9. **Prepare for Baking:**
   - Brush the top of the loaf with beaten egg if using. Sprinkle with chopped rosemary or thyme if desired.
10. **Bake:**
    - Bake for 25-30 minutes, or until the bread is golden brown and sounds hollow when tapped.
11. **Cool:**
    - Allow the bread to cool on a wire rack before slicing.

Serving Suggestions:

- Enjoy with a spread of butter or a drizzle of olive oil.
- Excellent as a side for soups, salads, or alongside cheese.

Green Olive Bread is aromatic and flavorful, with the distinctive brininess of olives adding depth to each bite. It's a great way to elevate your bread routine with a Mediterranean twist. Enjoy baking and savoring this delicious bread!

Date and Nut Bread

Ingredients:

For the Dough:

- 1 cup dates, pitted and chopped
- 1 cup nuts (such as walnuts or pecans), chopped
- 1½ cups all-purpose flour
- 1½ cups whole wheat flour
- 1 packet (2¼ tsp) active dry yeast
- 1 cup warm water (110°F or 45°C)
- ¼ cup honey or maple syrup
- ¼ cup vegetable oil
- 1 tsp salt
- 1 tsp ground cinnamon (optional)

For the Topping (optional):

- 2 tbsp chopped nuts
- 2 tbsp honey or maple syrup (for drizzling)

Instructions:

1. **Prepare Dates and Nuts:**
    - In a small bowl, combine the chopped dates and nuts. Set aside.
2. **Activate the Yeast:**
    - In a small bowl, dissolve honey or maple syrup in warm water. Sprinkle yeast over and let it sit for 5-10 minutes until frothy.
3. **Mix the Dough:**
    - In a large bowl, combine all-purpose flour, whole wheat flour, salt, and ground cinnamon if using.
    - Add the yeast mixture and vegetable oil. Mix until a dough forms.
4. **Incorporate Dates and Nuts:**
    - Turn the dough onto a floured surface and knead for about 5 minutes.
    - Gently knead in the dates and nuts until evenly distributed.
5. **Knead:**
    - Continue kneading the dough for about 8-10 minutes, until smooth and elastic.
6. **First Rise:**
    - Place the dough in a lightly oiled bowl, cover with plastic wrap or a damp cloth, and let it rise in a warm place for about 1 hour, or until doubled in size.
7. **Shape the Bread:**

- Punch down the dough and turn it onto a floured surface. Shape into a loaf or divide into smaller pieces if making rolls.
- Place the shaped dough on a parchment-lined baking sheet or in a greased loaf pan.

8. **Second Rise:**
   - Cover the dough and let it rise for another 30-45 minutes, or until puffy.
9. **Preheat Oven:**
   - Preheat your oven to 375°F (190°C).
10. **Prepare for Baking:**
    - Brush the top of the loaf with honey or maple syrup if using. Sprinkle with additional chopped nuts if desired.
11. **Bake:**
    - Bake for 30-35 minutes, or until the bread is golden brown and sounds hollow when tapped.
12. **Cool:**
    - Allow the bread to cool on a wire rack before slicing.

Serving Suggestions:

- Enjoy sliced with a bit of butter or cream cheese.
- Great for breakfast, as a snack, or with tea.

Date and Nut Bread is sweet, nutty, and satisfying, making it a delicious choice for any time of day. Enjoy baking and savoring this hearty bread!

Coriander Flatbread

Ingredients:

For the Dough:

- 2 cups all-purpose flour
- 1 packet (2¼ tsp) active dry yeast
- 1 cup warm water (110°F or 45°C)
- 2 tbsp olive oil
- 1 tsp sugar
- 1½ tsp salt
- 2 tbsp coriander seeds, crushed or ground
- 1 tsp ground cumin (optional, for added flavor)

For the Topping (optional):

- 2 tbsp olive oil
- 1 tbsp sesame seeds or additional crushed coriander seeds
- Coarse sea salt

Instructions:

1. **Activate the Yeast:**
    - In a small bowl, dissolve sugar in warm water. Sprinkle yeast over and let it sit for 5-10 minutes until frothy.
2. **Mix the Dough:**
    - In a large bowl, combine flour, salt, crushed coriander seeds, and ground cumin if using.
    - Add the yeast mixture and olive oil. Mix until a dough forms.
3. **Knead:**
    - Turn the dough onto a floured surface and knead for about 5-7 minutes, until smooth and elastic.
4. **First Rise:**
    - Place the dough in a lightly oiled bowl, cover with plastic wrap or a damp cloth, and let it rise in a warm place for about 1 hour, or until doubled in size.
5. **Prepare for Shaping:**
    - Punch down the dough and turn it onto a floured surface. Divide into 4-6 pieces, depending on the size of the flatbreads you prefer.
    - Roll each piece into a thin, flat circle or oval, about ¼ inch thick.
6. **Preheat Oven:**
    - Preheat your oven to 475°F (245°C). If using a pizza stone, place it in the oven to preheat as well.

7. **Prepare the Flatbreads:**
    - Place the rolled-out dough onto a parchment-lined baking sheet or preheated pizza stone.
    - Brush the tops with olive oil and sprinkle with sesame seeds, additional crushed coriander seeds, and coarse sea salt.
8. **Bake:**
    - Bake for 8-10 minutes, or until the flatbreads are golden brown and crispy.
9. **Cool:**
    - Allow the flatbreads to cool slightly before slicing or serving.

Serving Suggestions:

- Serve with dips like hummus, tzatziki, or baba ganoush.
- Use as a base for various toppings or as a side to soups and salads.

Coriander Flatbread is aromatic and flavorful with a delightful crunch, making it a great addition to many meals. Enjoy baking and savoring this fragrant bread!

Sweet Potato Bread

Ingredients:

For the Dough:

- 1 cup mashed sweet potatoes (about 1 medium sweet potato)
- 4 cups all-purpose flour
- 1 packet (2¼ tsp) active dry yeast
- 1 cup warm milk (110°F or 45°C)
- ¼ cup honey or maple syrup
- ¼ cup vegetable oil
- 1 tsp salt
- 1 tsp ground cinnamon
- ½ tsp ground nutmeg (optional)
- ½ tsp ground ginger (optional)
- 2 large eggs

For the Topping (optional):

- 1 egg, beaten (for egg wash)
- 2 tbsp brown sugar or coarse sugar (for sprinkling)

Instructions:

1. **Prepare Sweet Potatoes:**
    - Bake or boil sweet potatoes until tender, then mash until smooth. Measure out 1 cup of mashed sweet potato and let it cool slightly.
2. **Activate the Yeast:**
    - In a small bowl, dissolve honey or maple syrup in warm milk. Sprinkle yeast over and let it sit for 5-10 minutes until frothy.
3. **Mix the Dough:**
    - In a large bowl, combine flour, salt, cinnamon, nutmeg, and ginger.
    - Add the yeast mixture, mashed sweet potato, vegetable oil, and eggs. Mix until a dough forms.
4. **Knead:**
    - Turn the dough onto a floured surface and knead for about 8-10 minutes, until smooth and elastic.
5. **First Rise:**
    - Place the dough in a lightly oiled bowl, cover with plastic wrap or a damp cloth, and let it rise in a warm place for about 1 hour, or until doubled in size.
6. **Shape the Bread:**

- Punch down the dough and turn it onto a floured surface. Shape into a loaf or divide into smaller pieces if making rolls.
- Place the shaped dough on a parchment-lined baking sheet or in a greased loaf pan.

7. **Second Rise:**
   - Cover the dough and let it rise for another 30-45 minutes, or until puffy.
8. **Preheat Oven:**
   - Preheat your oven to 375°F (190°C).
9. **Prepare for Baking:**
   - Brush the top of the loaf with beaten egg if using. Sprinkle with brown sugar or coarse sugar if desired.
10. **Bake:**
    - Bake for 30-35 minutes, or until the bread is golden brown and sounds hollow when tapped.
11. **Cool:**
    - Allow the bread to cool on a wire rack before slicing.

Serving Suggestions:

- Enjoy warm with a pat of butter.
- Great for breakfast or as a snack.

Sweet Potato Bread is moist and subtly sweet, with warm spices adding depth to its flavor. Enjoy your homemade bread!

Garlic Bread

Ingredients:

For the Bread:

- 1 loaf Italian or French bread
- ½ cup (1 stick) unsalted butter, softened
- 4-6 cloves garlic, minced
- 2 tbsp fresh parsley, chopped (or 1 tbsp dried parsley)
- ¼ tsp salt
- ¼ tsp ground black pepper
- ¼ tsp crushed red pepper flakes (optional, for a bit of heat)
- ¼ cup grated Parmesan cheese (optional, for added flavor)

Instructions:

1. **Preheat Oven:**
    - Preheat your oven to 375°F (190°C).
2. **Prepare the Garlic Butter:**
    - In a medium bowl, mix softened butter with minced garlic, parsley, salt, pepper, and crushed red pepper flakes if using. Stir until well combined.
3. **Prepare the Bread:**
    - Slice the loaf of bread in half lengthwise. You can also slice it into individual pieces if you prefer smaller servings.
4. **Spread the Garlic Butter:**
    - Spread the garlic butter mixture evenly over the cut sides of the bread.
5. **Add Parmesan (optional):**
    - If using Parmesan cheese, sprinkle it evenly over the buttered bread.
6. **Bake:**
    - Place the bread halves on a baking sheet, cut side up. Bake for 10-15 minutes, or until the edges are golden and the butter is melted. For a crispier top, broil for an additional 1-2 minutes, watching closely to avoid burning.
7. **Cool and Serve:**
    - Let the garlic bread cool slightly before slicing if you haven't already. Serve warm.

Serving Suggestions:

- Great as a side for pasta dishes, soups, or salads.
- Can be used to make garlic bread sandwiches.

Garlic Bread is a simple yet irresistible treat with its rich, buttery, and garlicky flavor. Enjoy!

Cinnamon Bread

Ingredients:

For the Dough:

- 3½ cups all-purpose flour
- 1 packet (2¼ tsp) active dry yeast
- 1 cup warm milk (110°F or 45°C)
- ¼ cup granulated sugar
- ¼ cup unsalted butter, softened
- 1 tsp salt
- 2 large eggs

For the Cinnamon Swirl:

- ½ cup granulated sugar
- 2 tbsp ground cinnamon
- 2 tbsp unsalted butter, melted

For the Glaze (optional):

- 1 cup powdered sugar
- 2 tbsp milk or cream
- ½ tsp vanilla extract

Instructions:

1. **Activate the Yeast:**
   - In a small bowl, dissolve ¼ cup sugar in warm milk. Sprinkle yeast over and let it sit for 5-10 minutes until frothy.
2. **Mix the Dough:**
   - In a large bowl, combine flour and salt.
   - Add the yeast mixture, softened butter, and eggs. Mix until a dough forms.
3. **Knead:**
   - Turn the dough onto a floured surface and knead for about 8-10 minutes, until smooth and elastic.
4. **First Rise:**
   - Place the dough in a lightly oiled bowl, cover with plastic wrap or a damp cloth, and let it rise in a warm place for about 1 hour, or until doubled in size.
5. **Prepare the Cinnamon Swirl:**
   - In a small bowl, mix together ½ cup sugar and 2 tbsp cinnamon.

- Punch down the dough and turn it onto a floured surface. Roll out into a rectangle about ¼ inch thick.
- Brush the dough with melted butter and sprinkle evenly with the cinnamon sugar mixture.

6. **Shape the Bread:**
   - Roll the dough up tightly from one end to form a log. Pinch the seams to seal.
   - Place the rolled dough into a greased loaf pan.
7. **Second Rise:**
   - Cover and let the dough rise for another 30-45 minutes, or until puffy.
8. **Preheat Oven:**
   - Preheat your oven to 350°F (175°C).
9. **Bake:**
   - Bake for 30-35 minutes, or until the bread is golden brown and sounds hollow when tapped.
10. **Cool and Glaze (optional):**
    - Let the bread cool in the pan for 10 minutes, then transfer to a wire rack to cool completely.
    - For the glaze, mix powdered sugar, milk, and vanilla extract until smooth. Drizzle over the cooled bread.

Serving Suggestions:

- Enjoy warm or at room temperature.
- Perfect for breakfast, a snack, or dessert.

Cinnamon Bread is sweet, comforting, and perfect for a cozy treat. Enjoy your baking!

Whole Wheat Pita

Ingredients:

For the Dough:

- 2 cups whole wheat flour
- 1 cup all-purpose flour
- 1 packet (2¼ tsp) active dry yeast
- 1 cup warm water (110°F or 45°C)
- 2 tbsp olive oil
- 1 tbsp honey or maple syrup
- 1 tsp salt

Instructions:

1. **Activate the Yeast:**
    - In a small bowl, dissolve honey or maple syrup in warm water. Sprinkle yeast over and let it sit for 5-10 minutes until frothy.
2. **Mix the Dough:**
    - In a large bowl, combine whole wheat flour, all-purpose flour, and salt.
    - Add the yeast mixture and olive oil. Mix until a dough forms.
3. **Knead:**
    - Turn the dough onto a floured surface and knead for about 8 minutes, until smooth and elastic.
4. **First Rise:**
    - Place the dough in a lightly oiled bowl, cover with plastic wrap or a damp cloth, and let it rise in a warm place for about 1 hour, or until doubled in size.
5. **Shape the Pitas:**
    - Punch down the dough and turn it onto a floured surface. Divide into 8 equal pieces.
    - Roll each piece into a circle about ¼ inch thick.
6. **Preheat Oven:**
    - Preheat your oven to 475°F (245°C). If using a pizza stone, place it in the oven to preheat as well.
7. **Bake:**
    - Place the rolled dough circles on a parchment-lined baking sheet or preheated pizza stone. Bake for 5-7 minutes, or until the pitas puff up and are lightly browned.
8. **Cool:**
    - Transfer the pitas to a wire rack to cool. They will deflate slightly as they cool, creating the classic pocket.

Serving Suggestions:

- Use for sandwiches, wraps, or as a side with dips like hummus or tzatziki.

Whole Wheat Pita Bread offers a nutritious twist on the traditional pita, with a deliciously nutty flavor and soft texture. Enjoy your homemade pitas!

Pumpkin Bread

Ingredients:

For the Bread:

- 1¾ cups all-purpose flour
- 1 cup granulated sugar
- ½ cup brown sugar, packed
- 1 tsp baking powder
- ½ tsp baking soda
- ½ tsp salt
- 1 tsp ground cinnamon
- ½ tsp ground nutmeg
- ¼ tsp ground ginger
- ¼ tsp ground cloves
- ½ cup vegetable oil or melted coconut oil
- 1 cup canned pumpkin puree (not pumpkin pie filling)
- 2 large eggs
- ¼ cup water or milk
- 1 tsp vanilla extract

For Optional Add-ins:

- ½ cup chopped walnuts or pecans
- ¼ cup chocolate chips or dried cranberries

For the Topping (optional):

- 2 tbsp granulated sugar
- 1 tsp ground cinnamon

Instructions:

1. **Preheat Oven:**
   - Preheat your oven to 350°F (175°C). Grease and flour a 9x5-inch loaf pan or line it with parchment paper.
2. **Mix Dry Ingredients:**
   - In a large bowl, whisk together flour, granulated sugar, brown sugar, baking powder, baking soda, salt, cinnamon, nutmeg, ginger, and cloves.
3. **Mix Wet Ingredients:**
   - In another bowl, combine the oil, pumpkin puree, eggs, water or milk, and vanilla extract. Whisk until well combined.

4. **Combine Ingredients:**
   - Add the wet ingredients to the dry ingredients and mix until just combined. Do not overmix. Fold in any optional add-ins like nuts or chocolate chips if using.
5. **Prepare the Loaf:**
   - Pour the batter into the prepared loaf pan and smooth the top.
6. **Optional Topping:**
   - If desired, mix 2 tbsp sugar with 1 tsp cinnamon and sprinkle over the top of the batter before baking.
7. **Bake:**
   - Bake for 55-65 minutes, or until a toothpick inserted into the center of the bread comes out clean. The top should be golden brown and the bread should feel firm to the touch.
8. **Cool:**
   - Allow the bread to cool in the pan for 10 minutes, then transfer to a wire rack to cool completely before slicing.

Serving Suggestions:

- Enjoy plain, or spread with a bit of butter or cream cheese.
- Great for breakfast, a snack, or dessert.

Pumpkin Bread is a delightful treat with its warm spices and moist texture. Enjoy baking and savoring this delicious fall favorite!

Caramelized Onion Bread

Ingredients:

For the Caramelized Onions:

- 2 large onions, thinly sliced
- 2 tbsp olive oil
- 1 tbsp unsalted butter
- 1 tsp sugar
- ¼ tsp salt

For the Dough:

- 3½ cups all-purpose flour
- 1 packet (2¼ tsp) active dry yeast
- 1½ cups warm water (110°F or 45°C)
- ¼ cup olive oil
- 1 tbsp honey
- 1½ tsp salt

Instructions:

1. **Caramelize the Onions:**
   - Heat olive oil and butter in a large skillet over medium heat.
   - Add the onions, sugar, and salt. Cook, stirring frequently, for 20-25 minutes until the onions are deeply browned and caramelized. Set aside to cool.
2. **Activate the Yeast:**
   - In a small bowl, dissolve honey in warm water. Sprinkle yeast over and let it sit for 5-10 minutes until frothy.
3. **Mix the Dough:**
   - In a large bowl, combine flour and salt.
   - Add the yeast mixture and olive oil. Mix until a dough forms.
4. **Knead:**
   - Turn the dough onto a floured surface and knead for about 8-10 minutes, until smooth and elastic.
5. **First Rise:**
   - Place the dough in a lightly oiled bowl, cover with plastic wrap or a damp cloth, and let it rise in a warm place for about 1 hour, or until doubled in size.
6. **Incorporate the Onions:**
   - Punch down the dough and turn it onto a floured surface. Gently knead in the caramelized onions until evenly distributed.
7. **Shape the Bread:**

- Shape the dough into a loaf and place it in a greased loaf pan or on a parchment-lined baking sheet.
8. **Second Rise:**
   - Cover and let the dough rise for another 30-45 minutes, or until puffy.
9. **Preheat Oven:**
   - Preheat your oven to 375°F (190°C).
10. **Bake:**
    - Bake for 30-35 minutes, or until the bread is golden brown and sounds hollow when tapped.
11. **Cool:**
    - Allow the bread to cool on a wire rack before slicing.

Serving Suggestions:

- Enjoy with butter or as a side to soups and salads.
- Great for making savory sandwiches or toast.

Caramelized Onion Bread is rich and flavorful, with a delightful sweetness from the onions. Enjoy baking and savoring this savory loaf!

Mediterranean Bread

Ingredients:

For the Dough:

- 3½ cups all-purpose flour
- 1 packet (2¼ tsp) active dry yeast
- 1½ cups warm water (110°F or 45°C)
- ¼ cup olive oil
- 1 tbsp honey
- 1½ tsp salt

For the Mix-ins:

- ½ cup kalamata olives, pitted and chopped
- ½ cup feta cheese, crumbled
- 2 tbsp fresh rosemary or thyme, chopped (or 1 tbsp dried)
- 2 tbsp sun-dried tomatoes, chopped (optional)
- ¼ cup chopped fresh parsley (optional)

Instructions:

1. **Activate the Yeast:**
   - In a small bowl, dissolve honey in warm water. Sprinkle yeast over and let it sit for 5-10 minutes until frothy.
2. **Mix the Dough:**
   - In a large bowl, combine flour and salt.
   - Add the yeast mixture and olive oil. Mix until a dough forms.
3. **Knead:**
   - Turn the dough onto a floured surface and knead for about 8-10 minutes, until smooth and elastic.
4. **Incorporate Mix-ins:**
   - Gently knead in olives, feta cheese, herbs, sun-dried tomatoes, and parsley if using, until evenly distributed.
5. **First Rise:**
   - Place the dough in a lightly oiled bowl, cover with plastic wrap or a damp cloth, and let it rise in a warm place for about 1 hour, or until doubled in size.
6. **Shape the Bread:**
   - Punch down the dough and turn it onto a floured surface. Shape into a loaf or divide into smaller pieces if making rolls.
7. **Second Rise:**

- Place the shaped dough on a parchment-lined baking sheet or in a greased loaf pan. Cover and let rise for another 30-45 minutes, or until puffy.
8. **Preheat Oven:**
    - Preheat your oven to 375°F (190°C).
9. **Bake:**
    - Bake for 30-35 minutes, or until the bread is golden brown and sounds hollow when tapped.
10. **Cool:**
    - Allow the bread to cool on a wire rack before slicing.

Serving Suggestions:

- Serve with olive oil for dipping or alongside Mediterranean dishes like hummus and tzatziki.
- Great for sandwiches or as a side to salads.

Mediterranean Bread is packed with savory flavors and makes a wonderful addition to any meal. Enjoy baking and savoring this delicious loaf!

Rosemary Focaccia

Ingredients:

For the Dough:

- 3½ cups all-purpose flour
- 1 packet (2¼ tsp) active dry yeast
- 1½ cups warm water (110°F or 45°C)
- ¼ cup olive oil (plus extra for drizzling)
- 1 tbsp honey
- 1½ tsp salt

For the Topping:

- 2-3 tbsp fresh rosemary leaves
- Coarse sea salt (to taste)
- 2-3 tbsp olive oil

Instructions:

1. **Activate the Yeast:**
   - In a small bowl, dissolve honey in warm water. Sprinkle yeast over and let it sit for 5-10 minutes until frothy.
2. **Mix the Dough:**
   - In a large bowl, combine flour and salt.
   - Add the yeast mixture and ¼ cup olive oil. Mix until a dough forms.
3. **Knead:**
   - Turn the dough onto a floured surface and knead for about 8-10 minutes, until smooth and elastic.
4. **First Rise:**
   - Place the dough in a lightly oiled bowl, cover with plastic wrap or a damp cloth, and let it rise in a warm place for about 1 hour, or until doubled in size.
5. **Prepare for Shaping:**
   - Punch down the dough and turn it onto a floured surface. Shape it into a rectangle and transfer it to a parchment-lined baking sheet or a greased baking pan.
6. **Second Rise:**
   - Use your fingers to dimple the dough all over. Cover and let rise for another 30 minutes, or until puffy.
7. **Preheat Oven:**
   - Preheat your oven to 425°F (220°C).
8. **Add Toppings:**

        - Drizzle olive oil over the top of the dough. Sprinkle with fresh rosemary leaves and coarse sea salt.
9. **Bake:**
        - Bake for 20-25 minutes, or until the focaccia is golden brown and has a crisp crust.
10. **Cool:**
        - Allow the focaccia to cool slightly on a wire rack before slicing.

Serving Suggestions:

- Serve warm as an appetizer or side dish.
- Excellent with olive oil for dipping or alongside soups and salads.

Rosemary Focaccia is aromatic and delicious, with a crispy crust and a soft, airy interior. Enjoy your homemade bread!

Lavash

Ingredients:

- 2¼ cups all-purpose flour
- 1 packet (2¼ tsp) active dry yeast
- 1 cup warm water (110°F or 45°C)
- 2 tbsp olive oil
- 1 tsp sugar
- 1 tsp salt

Instructions:

1. **Activate the Yeast:**
   - In a small bowl, dissolve sugar in warm water. Sprinkle yeast over and let it sit for 5-10 minutes until frothy.
2. **Mix the Dough:**
   - In a large bowl, combine flour and salt.
   - Add the yeast mixture and olive oil. Mix until a dough forms.
3. **Knead:**
   - Turn the dough onto a floured surface and knead for about 5-7 minutes, until smooth and elastic.
4. **First Rise:**
   - Place the dough in a lightly oiled bowl, cover with plastic wrap or a damp cloth, and let it rise in a warm place for about 1 hour, or until doubled in size.
5. **Prepare for Shaping:**
   - Punch down the dough and turn it onto a floured surface. Divide into 4-6 equal portions.
6. **Roll Out:**
   - Roll each portion into a thin rectangle or oval, about ⅛ inch thick. Try to roll it out as evenly as possible.
7. **Preheat Oven:**
   - Preheat your oven to 475°F (245°C). If you have a baking stone, place it in the oven to preheat as well.
8. **Bake:**
   - Place the rolled-out dough onto a parchment-lined baking sheet or preheated baking stone.
   - Bake for 4-6 minutes, or until the lavash is lightly golden and crisp.
9. **Cool:**
   - Allow the lavash to cool slightly on a wire rack before using.

Serving Suggestions:

- Use lavash for wraps or sandwiches.
- Cut into pieces and serve with dips like hummus or baba ganoush.
- Top with cheese and herbs, then bake for a quick flatbread.

Lavash is versatile and can be used in various ways, from wraps to crispy snacks. Enjoy your homemade lavash!

Sun-Dried Tomato Bread

Ingredients:

For the Dough:

- 3½ cups all-purpose flour
- 1 packet (2¼ tsp) active dry yeast
- 1½ cups warm water (110°F or 45°C)
- ¼ cup olive oil
- 1 tbsp honey
- 1½ tsp salt

For the Mix-ins:

- ½ cup sun-dried tomatoes, chopped (preferably packed in oil, drained)
- ¼ cup fresh basil or parsley, chopped (or 1 tbsp dried)
- ¼ cup grated Parmesan cheese (optional)

Instructions:

1. **Activate the Yeast:**
    - In a small bowl, dissolve honey in warm water. Sprinkle yeast over and let it sit for 5-10 minutes until frothy.
2. **Mix the Dough:**
    - In a large bowl, combine flour and salt.
    - Add the yeast mixture and olive oil. Mix until a dough forms.
3. **Knead:**
    - Turn the dough onto a floured surface and knead for about 8-10 minutes, until smooth and elastic.
4. **Incorporate Mix-ins:**
    - Gently knead in the sun-dried tomatoes, basil or parsley, and Parmesan cheese if using, until evenly distributed.
5. **First Rise:**
    - Place the dough in a lightly oiled bowl, cover with plastic wrap or a damp cloth, and let it rise in a warm place for about 1 hour, or until doubled in size.
6. **Shape the Bread:**
    - Punch down the dough and turn it onto a floured surface. Shape it into a loaf or divide into smaller pieces if making rolls.
7. **Second Rise:**
    - Place the shaped dough on a parchment-lined baking sheet or in a greased loaf pan. Cover and let rise for another 30-45 minutes, or until puffy.
8. **Preheat Oven:**

- Preheat your oven to 375°F (190°C).
9. **Bake:**
   - Bake for 30-35 minutes, or until the bread is golden brown and sounds hollow when tapped.
10. **Cool:**
    - Allow the bread to cool on a wire rack before slicing.

Serving Suggestions:

- Delicious on its own, or served with cheese and olives.
- Great for making sandwiches or as an accompaniment to soups.

Sun-Dried Tomato Bread adds a burst of flavor to any meal with its rich tomato and herb notes. Enjoy baking and savoring this delightful loaf!

Coconut Bread

Ingredients:

For the Dough:

- 3½ cups all-purpose flour
- 1 packet (2¼ tsp) active dry yeast
- 1½ cups warm water (110°F or 45°C)
- ¼ cup olive oil
- 1 tbsp honey
- 1½ tsp salt

For the Mix-ins:

- ½ cup sun-dried tomatoes, chopped (preferably packed in oil, drained)
- ¼ cup fresh basil or parsley, chopped (or 1 tbsp dried)
- ¼ cup grated Parmesan cheese (optional)

Instructions:

1. **Activate the Yeast:**
    - In a small bowl, dissolve honey in warm water. Sprinkle yeast over and let it sit for 5-10 minutes until frothy.
2. **Mix the Dough:**
    - In a large bowl, combine flour and salt.
    - Add the yeast mixture and olive oil. Mix until a dough forms.
3. **Knead:**
    - Turn the dough onto a floured surface and knead for about 8-10 minutes, until smooth and elastic.
4. **Incorporate Mix-ins:**
    - Gently knead in the sun-dried tomatoes, basil or parsley, and Parmesan cheese if using, until evenly distributed.
5. **First Rise:**
    - Place the dough in a lightly oiled bowl, cover with plastic wrap or a damp cloth, and let it rise in a warm place for about 1 hour, or until doubled in size.
6. **Shape the Bread:**
    - Punch down the dough and turn it onto a floured surface. Shape it into a loaf or divide into smaller pieces if making rolls.
7. **Second Rise:**
    - Place the shaped dough on a parchment-lined baking sheet or in a greased loaf pan. Cover and let rise for another 30-45 minutes, or until puffy.
8. **Preheat Oven:**

- Preheat your oven to 375°F (190°C).
9. **Bake:**
    - Bake for 30-35 minutes, or until the bread is golden brown and sounds hollow when tapped.
10. **Cool:**
    - Allow the bread to cool on a wire rack before slicing.

Serving Suggestions:

- Delicious on its own, or served with cheese and olives.
- Great for making sandwiches or as an accompaniment to soups.

Sun-Dried Tomato Bread adds a burst of flavor to any meal with its rich tomato and herb notes. Enjoy baking and savoring this delightful loaf!

Coconut Bread

Ingredients:

For the Dough:

- 2 cups all-purpose flour
- 1 cup shredded unsweetened coconut
- ½ cup granulated sugar
- 1 tsp baking powder
- ½ tsp baking soda
- ¼ tsp salt
- ½ cup coconut oil (or vegetable oil)
- 1 cup canned coconut milk (full-fat)
- 2 large eggs
- 1 tsp vanilla extract

For Optional Topping:

- ¼ cup shredded coconut (sweetened or unsweetened)
- 1 tbsp granulated sugar

Instructions:

1. **Preheat Oven:**
   - Preheat your oven to 350°F (175°C). Grease and flour a 9x5-inch loaf pan or line it with parchment paper.
2. **Mix Dry Ingredients:**
   - In a large bowl, whisk together flour, shredded coconut, sugar, baking powder, baking soda, and salt.
3. **Mix Wet Ingredients:**
   - In another bowl, whisk together the coconut oil, coconut milk, eggs, and vanilla extract until well combined.
4. **Combine Ingredients:**
   - Add the wet ingredients to the dry ingredients and mix until just combined. Be careful not to overmix.
5. **Pour and Smooth:**
   - Pour the batter into the prepared loaf pan and smooth the top with a spatula.
6. **Add Topping (optional):**
   - If using, sprinkle the top of the batter with shredded coconut and granulated sugar for a bit of extra texture and sweetness.
7. **Bake:**

- Bake for 50-60 minutes, or until a toothpick inserted into the center of the bread comes out clean and the top is golden brown.
8. **Cool:**
    - Allow the bread to cool in the pan for about 10 minutes, then transfer to a wire rack to cool completely before slicing.

Serving Suggestions:

- Enjoy plain or with a pat of butter.
- Great for breakfast or a mid-day snack.

Coconut Bread is rich, moist, and full of coconut flavor. Enjoy making and tasting this delightful loaf!

Sourdough Pita

Ingredients:

For the Dough:

- 1 cup active sourdough starter (fed and bubbly)
- 1½ cups warm water (110°F or 45°C)
- 4 cups all-purpose flour
- 1 tsp salt
- 1 tbsp olive oil
- 1 tsp honey (optional, for a touch of sweetness)

Instructions:

1. **Prepare the Dough:**
   - In a large bowl, mix the sourdough starter with warm water and honey (if using).
2. **Add Flour and Salt:**
   - Gradually add flour and salt to the starter mixture. Mix until a dough begins to form.
3. **Knead:**
   - Turn the dough onto a floured surface and knead for about 8-10 minutes until smooth and elastic.
4. **First Rise:**
   - Place the dough in a lightly oiled bowl, cover with plastic wrap or a damp cloth, and let it rise in a warm place for about 2-3 hours, or until doubled in size.
5. **Divide and Shape:**
   - Punch down the dough and turn it onto a floured surface. Divide into 8-10 equal pieces. Roll each piece into a thin circle about ¼ inch thick.
6. **Preheat Oven:**
   - Preheat your oven to 475°F (245°C). If using a pizza stone, place it in the oven to preheat as well.
7. **Bake:**
   - Place the rolled-out dough circles on a parchment-lined baking sheet or preheated pizza stone. Bake for 5-7 minutes, or until the pitas puff up and are lightly golden.
8. **Cool:**
   - Transfer the pitas to a wire rack to cool. They will deflate slightly as they cool, forming the classic pocket.

Serving Suggestions:

- Use for sandwiches, wraps, or as a side with dips like hummus.

- Great for making stuffed pitas or flatbread pizzas.

Sourdough Pita combines the classic pita texture with the tangy flavor of sourdough. Enjoy your homemade pita bread!

Quinoa Bread

Ingredients:

For the Dough:

- 1 cup cooked quinoa (cooled)
- 1¾ cups all-purpose flour (or whole wheat flour for a heartier loaf)
- 1 cup bread flour
- 1 packet (2¼ tsp) active dry yeast
- 1 cup warm water (110°F or 45°C)
- ¼ cup olive oil
- 2 tbsp honey or maple syrup
- 1½ tsp salt
- 1 large egg (optional, for enriched dough)

For Optional Add-ins:

- ¼ cup sunflower seeds or pumpkin seeds
- ¼ cup chopped nuts (such as walnuts or almonds)

Instructions:

1. **Prepare the Yeast:**
    - In a small bowl, dissolve honey or maple syrup in warm water. Sprinkle yeast over and let it sit for 5-10 minutes until frothy.
2. **Mix the Dough:**
    - In a large bowl, combine all-purpose flour, bread flour, and salt.
    - Add the yeast mixture, olive oil, and cooled quinoa. Mix until a dough forms. If using, beat in the egg at this stage.
3. **Knead:**
    - Turn the dough onto a floured surface and knead for about 8-10 minutes, until smooth and elastic.
4. **First Rise:**
    - Place the dough in a lightly oiled bowl, cover with plastic wrap or a damp cloth, and let it rise in a warm place for about 1-2 hours, or until doubled in size.
5. **Shape the Bread:**
    - Punch down the dough and turn it onto a floured surface. Shape it into a loaf and place it in a greased 9x5-inch loaf pan. If adding seeds or nuts, gently fold them into the dough before shaping.
6. **Second Rise:**
    - Cover and let the dough rise for another 30-45 minutes, or until puffy.
7. **Preheat Oven:**

- Preheat your oven to 375°F (190°C).
8. **Bake:**
   - Bake for 30-35 minutes, or until the bread is golden brown and sounds hollow when tapped. The internal temperature should be around 190°F (88°C).
9. **Cool:**
   - Allow the bread to cool in the pan for about 10 minutes, then transfer to a wire rack to cool completely before slicing.

Serving Suggestions:

- Enjoy toasted with a bit of butter or jam.
- Great for sandwiches or as a side to soups and salads.

Quinoa Bread is nutritious, with a great texture and flavor thanks to the quinoa. Enjoy making and eating this wholesome loaf!

Poppy Seed Challah

Ingredients:

For the Dough:

- 1 cup warm water (110°F or 45°C)
- 1 packet (2¼ tsp) active dry yeast
- ¼ cup honey
- 1/3 cup vegetable oil or canola oil
- 3 large eggs
- 4 cups all-purpose flour
- 1½ tsp salt

For the Topping:

- 1 egg, beaten (for egg wash)
- 2-3 tbsp poppy seeds

Instructions:

1. **Activate the Yeast:**
   - In a small bowl, dissolve honey in warm water. Sprinkle yeast over the top and let it sit for 5-10 minutes until frothy.
2. **Mix the Dough:**
   - In a large bowl, combine flour and salt.
   - Add the yeast mixture, oil, and eggs. Mix until a dough forms.
3. **Knead:**
   - Turn the dough onto a floured surface and knead for about 8-10 minutes, until smooth and elastic.
4. **First Rise:**
   - Place the dough in a lightly oiled bowl, cover with plastic wrap or a damp cloth, and let it rise in a warm place for about 1-2 hours, or until doubled in size.
5. **Shape the Challah:**
   - Punch down the dough and turn it onto a floured surface. Divide into three equal parts and roll each into a long rope.
   - Braid the ropes together to form a loaf, pinching the ends together to seal.
6. **Second Rise:**
   - Place the braided loaf on a parchment-lined baking sheet. Cover and let rise for another 30-45 minutes, or until puffy.
7. **Preheat Oven:**
   - Preheat your oven to 375°F (190°C).
8. **Apply Topping:**

    - Brush the loaf with the beaten egg and sprinkle generously with poppy seeds.
9. **Bake:**
    - Bake for 30-35 minutes, or until the challah is golden brown and sounds hollow when tapped.
10. **Cool:**
    - Allow the challah to cool on a wire rack before slicing.

Serving Suggestions:

- Perfect for serving with butter or honey.
- Delicious for sandwiches or as a sweet treat.

Poppy Seed Challah combines a classic braided structure with a delightful poppy seed topping, making it both beautiful and tasty. Enjoy your baking!

Kamut Bread

Ingredients:

For the Dough:

- 2 cups Kamut flour
- 1 cup all-purpose flour (or whole wheat flour for a more rustic texture)
- 1 packet (2¼ tsp) active dry yeast
- 1 cup warm water (110°F or 45°C)
- ¼ cup olive oil
- 2 tbsp honey or maple syrup
- 1½ tsp salt

For Optional Add-ins:

- ¼ cup sunflower seeds or pumpkin seeds
- ¼ cup chopped nuts (such as walnuts or almonds)

Instructions:

1. **Activate the Yeast:**
   - In a small bowl, dissolve honey or maple syrup in warm water. Sprinkle yeast over and let it sit for 5-10 minutes until frothy.
2. **Mix the Dough:**
   - In a large bowl, combine Kamut flour, all-purpose flour, and salt.
   - Add the yeast mixture and olive oil. Mix until a dough forms.
3. **Knead:**
   - Turn the dough onto a floured surface and knead for about 8-10 minutes, until smooth and elastic. If adding seeds or nuts, gently fold them into the dough during the last few minutes of kneading.
4. **First Rise:**
   - Place the dough in a lightly oiled bowl, cover with plastic wrap or a damp cloth, and let it rise in a warm place for about 1-2 hours, or until doubled in size.
5. **Shape the Bread:**
   - Punch down the dough and turn it onto a floured surface. Shape it into a loaf and place it in a greased 9x5-inch loaf pan. Alternatively, shape into a round or oval loaf and place on a parchment-lined baking sheet.
6. **Second Rise:**
   - Cover and let the dough rise for another 30-45 minutes, or until puffy.
7. **Preheat Oven:**
   - Preheat your oven to 375°F (190°C).
8. **Bake:**

         - Bake for 30-35 minutes, or until the bread is golden brown and sounds hollow when tapped. The internal temperature should be around 190°F (88°C).
9. **Cool:**
         - Allow the bread to cool in the pan for about 10 minutes, then transfer to a wire rack to cool completely before slicing.

Serving Suggestions:

- Enjoy with a pat of butter or a drizzle of honey.
- Excellent for sandwiches or as a side to soups and salads.

Kamut Bread offers a unique flavor profile with its nutty undertones and is a nutritious alternative to regular bread. Enjoy making and eating this wholesome loaf!

Zucchini Bread

Ingredients:

For the Bread:

- 1½ cups all-purpose flour
- 1½ tsp baking powder
- ½ tsp baking soda
- ½ tsp salt
- 1 tsp ground cinnamon
- ¼ tsp ground nutmeg (optional)
- 1 cup granulated sugar
- ½ cup vegetable oil or melted coconut oil
- 2 large eggs
- 1 tsp vanilla extract
- 1 cup grated zucchini (about 1 medium zucchini, unpeeled and squeezed to remove excess moisture)
- ½ cup chopped nuts (such as walnuts or pecans) or chocolate chips (optional)

For Optional Topping:

- 1 tbsp granulated sugar
- 1 tsp ground cinnamon

Instructions:

1. **Preheat Oven:**
   - Preheat your oven to 350°F (175°C). Grease and flour a 9x5-inch loaf pan or line it with parchment paper.
2. **Mix Dry Ingredients:**
   - In a medium bowl, whisk together flour, baking powder, baking soda, salt, cinnamon, and nutmeg (if using).
3. **Mix Wet Ingredients:**
   - In a large bowl, beat together sugar, oil, eggs, and vanilla extract until well combined.
4. **Combine Ingredients:**
   - Gradually add the dry ingredients to the wet ingredients, mixing just until combined. Avoid overmixing.
   - Gently fold in the grated zucchini and nuts or chocolate chips if using.
5. **Pour and Smooth:**
   - Pour the batter into the prepared loaf pan and smooth the top with a spatula.
6. **Add Topping (optional):**

- If desired, mix 1 tbsp sugar with 1 tsp cinnamon and sprinkle over the top of the batter.
7. **Bake:**
   - Bake for 50-60 minutes, or until a toothpick inserted into the center comes out clean and the bread is golden brown.
8. **Cool:**
   - Allow the bread to cool in the pan for about 10 minutes, then transfer to a wire rack to cool completely before slicing.

Serving Suggestions:

- Enjoy plain or with a smear of cream cheese or butter.
- Delicious as a breakfast item or a mid-day snack.

Zucchini Bread is wonderfully moist and slightly sweet, making it a favorite for both kids and adults. Enjoy baking and savoring this delightful bread!

Sweet Cornbread

Ingredients:

- 1 cup all-purpose flour
- 1 cup cornmeal
- ¼ cup granulated sugar
- 1 tbsp baking powder
- ½ tsp salt
- 1 cup milk (whole or buttermilk)
- 2 large eggs
- ¼ cup unsalted butter, melted (or vegetable oil)
- 1 cup fresh or frozen corn kernels (optional for added texture)

Instructions:

1. **Preheat Oven:**
   - Preheat your oven to 400°F (200°C). Grease an 8x8-inch baking dish or a 9-inch round cake pan. You can also use a cast-iron skillet for a crispy crust.
2. **Mix Dry Ingredients:**
   - In a large bowl, whisk together flour, cornmeal, sugar, baking powder, and salt.
3. **Mix Wet Ingredients:**
   - In another bowl, combine milk, eggs, and melted butter. If using, stir in the corn kernels.
4. **Combine Ingredients:**
   - Pour the wet ingredients into the dry ingredients and stir until just combined. The batter will be slightly lumpy, but don't overmix.
5. **Pour and Smooth:**
   - Pour the batter into the prepared baking dish or skillet and smooth the top with a spatula.
6. **Bake:**
   - Bake for 20-25 minutes, or until the top is golden brown and a toothpick inserted into the center comes out clean.
7. **Cool:**
   - Allow the cornbread to cool slightly before slicing. It's best served warm.

Serving Suggestions:

- Delicious on its own or with a pat of butter.
- Pairs wonderfully with chili, soups, or as a side dish with barbecue.

Sweet Cornbread is a comforting and versatile bread with a touch of sweetness and a tender crumb. Enjoy baking and savoring this classic favorite!

Crispy Flatbread

Ingredients:

- 1½ cups all-purpose flour
- 1 tsp baking powder
- ½ tsp salt
- ¼ cup olive oil (plus extra for brushing)
- ½ cup warm water (110°F or 45°C)
- 1 tsp dried herbs (optional, such as rosemary, thyme, or oregano)
- Coarse sea salt for sprinkling (optional)

Instructions:

1. **Preheat Oven:**
   - Preheat your oven to 450°F (230°C). If using a baking stone, place it in the oven to preheat as well.
2. **Mix Dry Ingredients:**
   - In a large bowl, whisk together flour, baking powder, and salt. If using dried herbs, add them to the dry ingredients.
3. **Add Wet Ingredients:**
   - Make a well in the center of the dry ingredients and add the olive oil and warm water. Mix until a dough forms.
4. **Knead:**
   - Turn the dough onto a floured surface and knead gently for about 1-2 minutes until smooth.
5. **Roll Out:**
   - Divide the dough into 2-4 equal pieces. Roll each piece out into a thin rectangle or circle, about ¼ inch thick. The thinner you roll the dough, the crispier the flatbread will be.
6. **Prepare for Baking:**
   - Transfer the rolled-out dough to a parchment-lined baking sheet or directly onto the preheated baking stone if using. Brush the top with a little olive oil and sprinkle with coarse sea salt if desired.
7. **Bake:**
   - Bake for 8-10 minutes, or until the flatbread is golden brown and crispy. Keep an eye on it to avoid burning, as baking times may vary depending on your oven and the thickness of the dough.
8. **Cool:**
   - Remove the flatbread from the oven and let it cool slightly on a wire rack before breaking or cutting into pieces.

Serving Suggestions:

- Serve with dips like hummus, tzatziki, or salsa.
- Use as a base for flatbread pizzas or as a side with soups and salads.

Crispy Flatbread is incredibly versatile and can be customized with your favorite herbs and seasonings. Enjoy making and munching on this delightful bread!

Herbed Focaccia

Ingredients:

For the Dough:

- 3½ cups all-purpose flour
- 1 packet (2¼ tsp) active dry yeast
- 1½ cups warm water (110°F or 45°C)
- ¼ cup olive oil (plus extra for drizzling)
- 2 tsp salt
- 1 tbsp honey or sugar

For the Topping:

- 2-3 tbsp olive oil
- 2-3 cloves garlic, thinly sliced
- 2 tbsp fresh rosemary or thyme (or 1 tbsp dried)
- Coarse sea salt for sprinkling

Instructions:

1. **Prepare the Yeast:**
   - In a small bowl, dissolve honey or sugar in warm water. Sprinkle yeast over the top and let it sit for 5-10 minutes until frothy.
2. **Mix the Dough:**
   - In a large bowl, combine flour and salt. Add the yeast mixture and olive oil. Mix until a dough forms.
3. **Knead:**
   - Turn the dough onto a floured surface and knead for about 8-10 minutes, until smooth and elastic.
4. **First Rise:**
   - Place the dough in a lightly oiled bowl, cover with plastic wrap or a damp cloth, and let it rise in a warm place for about 1-2 hours, or until doubled in size.
5. **Shape and Second Rise:**
   - Punch down the dough and transfer it to a well-oiled 9x13-inch baking pan. Spread it out to fit the pan, and use your fingers to dimple the surface. Cover and let it rise for another 30-45 minutes.
6. **Prepare Topping:**
   - Preheat your oven to 425°F (220°C). Drizzle the risen dough with olive oil. Scatter sliced garlic and herbs over the top, and sprinkle with coarse sea salt.
7. **Bake:**

- Bake for 20-25 minutes, or until the focaccia is golden brown and crisp on the edges.
8. **Cool:**
    - Allow the focaccia to cool slightly on a wire rack before cutting into pieces.

Serving Suggestions:

- Delicious on its own or served with olive oil and balsamic vinegar for dipping.
- Great as a side with soups, salads, or for making sandwiches.

Herbed Focaccia is aromatic and flavorful, making it a delightful addition to any meal. Enjoy your baking!

Spelt Bread

Ingredients:

For the Dough:

- 2 cups spelt flour
- 1 cup all-purpose flour (or whole wheat flour for a denser loaf)
- 1 packet (2¼ tsp) active dry yeast
- 1 cup warm water (110°F or 45°C)
- ¼ cup honey or maple syrup
- ¼ cup olive oil
- 1½ tsp salt

Instructions:

1. **Prepare the Yeast:**
    - In a small bowl, dissolve honey or maple syrup in warm water. Sprinkle yeast over the top and let it sit for 5-10 minutes until frothy.
2. **Mix the Dough:**
    - In a large bowl, combine spelt flour, all-purpose flour, and salt.
    - Add the yeast mixture and olive oil. Mix until a dough forms.
3. **Knead:**
    - Turn the dough onto a floured surface and knead for about 8-10 minutes, until smooth and elastic.
4. **First Rise:**
    - Place the dough in a lightly oiled bowl, cover with plastic wrap or a damp cloth, and let it rise in a warm place for about 1-2 hours, or until doubled in size.
5. **Shape the Bread:**
    - Punch down the dough and turn it onto a floured surface. Shape it into a loaf and place it in a greased 9x5-inch loaf pan, or shape it into a round loaf and place on a parchment-lined baking sheet.
6. **Second Rise:**
    - Cover and let the dough rise for another 30-45 minutes, or until puffy.
7. **Preheat Oven:**
    - Preheat your oven to 375°F (190°C).
8. **Bake:**
    - Bake for 30-35 minutes, or until the bread is golden brown and sounds hollow when tapped. The internal temperature should be around 190°F (88°C).
9. **Cool:**
    - Allow the bread to cool in the pan for about 10 minutes, then transfer to a wire rack to cool completely before slicing.

Serving Suggestions:

- Enjoy with butter, cheese, or your favorite spreads.
- Great for sandwiches or as a side with soups and salads.

Spelt Bread offers a nutty flavor and a tender crumb, making it a nutritious alternative to traditional bread. Enjoy baking and savoring this wholesome loaf!

Olive Bread

Ingredients:

For the Dough:

- 3½ cups all-purpose flour
- 1 packet (2¼ tsp) active dry yeast
- 1½ cups warm water (110°F or 45°C)
- ¼ cup olive oil
- 1½ tsp salt
- 1 tbsp honey or sugar (optional, for added flavor)
- 1 cup pitted olives, chopped (black, green, or a mix)

For Optional Topping:

- 1 tbsp olive oil
- Coarse sea salt for sprinkling
- 1-2 tbsp chopped fresh rosemary or thyme (optional)

Instructions:

1. **Prepare the Yeast:**
   - In a small bowl, dissolve honey or sugar in warm water. Sprinkle yeast over the top and let it sit for 5-10 minutes until frothy.
2. **Mix the Dough:**
   - In a large bowl, combine flour and salt.
   - Add the yeast mixture and olive oil. Mix until a dough forms.
3. **Knead:**
   - Turn the dough onto a floured surface and knead for about 8-10 minutes, until smooth and elastic.
4. **Incorporate Olives:**
   - Gently fold the chopped olives into the dough during the last few minutes of kneading.
5. **First Rise:**
   - Place the dough in a lightly oiled bowl, cover with plastic wrap or a damp cloth, and let it rise in a warm place for about 1-2 hours, or until doubled in size.
6. **Shape the Bread:**
   - Punch down the dough and turn it onto a floured surface. Shape it into a loaf and place it in a greased 9x5-inch loaf pan, or shape it into a round or oval loaf and place on a parchment-lined baking sheet.
7. **Second Rise:**
   - Cover and let the dough rise for another 30-45 minutes, or until puffy.

8. **Preheat Oven:**
    - Preheat your oven to 375°F (190°C).
9. **Prepare for Baking:**
    - Brush the top of the loaf with olive oil. Sprinkle with coarse sea salt and fresh rosemary or thyme if desired.
10. **Bake:**
    - Bake for 30-35 minutes, or until the bread is golden brown and sounds hollow when tapped. The internal temperature should be around 190°F (88°C).
11. **Cool:**
    - Allow the bread to cool in the pan for about 10 minutes, then transfer to a wire rack to cool completely before slicing.

Serving Suggestions:

- Delicious served warm or at room temperature.
- Great with cheese, salads, or as a side to soups.

Olive Bread is aromatic and flavorful, with the olives adding a savory depth that makes it a standout addition to any meal. Enjoy making and savoring this delightful bread!

Almond Bread

Ingredients:

For the Dough:

- 1½ cups all-purpose flour
- 1 cup almond flour
- 1 packet (2¼ tsp) active dry yeast
- 1 cup warm water (110°F or 45°C)
- ¼ cup honey or maple syrup
- ¼ cup olive oil or melted butter
- 1 tsp salt
- 1 large egg

For Optional Topping:

- ¼ cup sliced almonds
- 1 tbsp honey (for drizzling)

Instructions:

1. **Prepare the Yeast:**
    - In a small bowl, dissolve honey or maple syrup in warm water. Sprinkle yeast over the top and let it sit for 5-10 minutes until frothy.
2. **Mix the Dough:**
    - In a large bowl, combine all-purpose flour, almond flour, and salt.
    - Add the yeast mixture, olive oil or melted butter, and egg. Mix until a dough forms.
3. **Knead:**
    - Turn the dough onto a floured surface and knead for about 8-10 minutes, until smooth and elastic.
4. **First Rise:**
    - Place the dough in a lightly oiled bowl, cover with plastic wrap or a damp cloth, and let it rise in a warm place for about 1-2 hours, or until doubled in size.
5. **Shape the Bread:**
    - Punch down the dough and turn it onto a floured surface. Shape it into a loaf and place it in a greased 9x5-inch loaf pan, or shape it into a round or oval loaf and place on a parchment-lined baking sheet.
6. **Second Rise:**
    - Cover and let the dough rise for another 30-45 minutes, or until puffy.
7. **Preheat Oven:**
    - Preheat your oven to 375°F (190°C).

8. **Prepare for Baking:**
   - Brush the top of the loaf with a little water or additional honey if desired. Sprinkle sliced almonds over the top.
9. **Bake:**
   - Bake for 30-35 minutes, or until the bread is golden brown and sounds hollow when tapped. The internal temperature should be around 190°F (88°C).
10. **Cool:**
    - Allow the bread to cool in the pan for about 10 minutes, then transfer to a wire rack to cool completely before slicing.

Serving Suggestions:

- Enjoy toasted with butter or jam.
- Great for sandwiches or as a base for nut butter spreads.

Almond Bread has a lovely nutty flavor and a tender crumb, making it a delightful addition to your baking repertoire. Enjoy!

www.ingramcontent.com/pod-product-compliance
Lightning Source LLC
LaVergne TN
LVHW081602060526
838201LV00054B/2038